# Insho...
# the Carolinas' Coasts

*Finding and Catching*
*the Most Popular Salt-Water Game Fish*

By Bob Newman

Illustrated by Susan Newman
With Photographs by the Author

Down Home Press, Asheboro, N.C.

ISBN 1-878086-27-8

Library of Congress Number 94-070668

Printed in the United States of America

Cover Design by Ginger F. Harris
Book Design by Ginger F. Harris

2 3 4 5 6 7 8 9 10

Down Home Press
PO Box 4126
Asheboro, N.C. 27204

*For Susan*

# Acknowledgements

I would like to thank George Misko, a fishing friend that I am fortunate to have, for the many excursions and fish we have shared over the years.

Also on the 'thank you' list are my mentor, David E. Petzal, executive editor at *Field & Stream*; Dennis Adams for the comradeship; John Shesler for the bluefishing lessons; Jesse and The Colonel down at the trout hole; and the countless anglers who were kind enough to look the other way as I stole their fishing secrets.

My editor, Jerry Bledsoe, was crafty enough to recognize a good idea when he saw one, and turn it into a book worth reading.

My daughter and fishing buddy, Britta, for reteaching me about enthusiasm.

And of course my wife, Susan, for grinning and bearing it, and for the exquisite illustrations you see in these pages.

Many sincere thanks to you all.

# Introduction

The Carolinas are to salt-water anglers what South Dakota is to ring-necked pheasant hunters and Alaska is to salmon enthusiasts.

Few regions offer the remarkable variety and populations of fishes found off of the beaches, in the rivers, creeks, estuaries and inlets, around the piers and jetties, and in the lagoons and sounds of North and South Carolina.

From the mighty tarpon to the nerve-shattering bluefish; from the powerful red drum to the scrappy flounder; from the spunky sheepshead to the beautiful spotted seatrout; the inshore waters of the Carolinas' coasts are home to a wealth of strong, aggressive, and outright ornery game fish that draw countless thousands of anglers from near and far hoping to wrestle a giant "bull" red, lay into a 50-pound "smoker" king mackerel, battle an angry bluefish, or put a hefty black drum to the test.

What's more, Carolina inshore waters offer year-round action. Starting with the departing cold winds of winter, the beaches heat up in the spring with drum and bluefish action, and the rivers come alive with spotted seatrout, or "specks." As spring fades, the colorful and delicious spanish mackerel show up, as do the bigger king mackerel and flounder. Mid-summer finds huge tarpon prowling the sounds and outsized cobia hanging around buoys and flotsam near shore. As autumn approaches, the drum and blues return to the surf again to challenge anglers along the beaches, jetties, and piers. Winter brings slower action, but blues, stripers, and the occasional big drum will still be caught by anglers who know what to fish when, where, and how.

Less glorious fish than those mentioned—but fish that are nonetheless tasty and fun to catch—are taken from spring through fall. These include pompano, gray trout, whiting, croaker, spots, and sea mullet. But there's more.

In the brackish waters of rivers and creeks, anglers find largemouth bass, "jack" (chain pickerel), catfish, and even gar that put a new perspective on "inshore" fishing.

But why this book?

Well, to tell the truth, this book came about as a result of frustration. I am a U.S. Marine, and the Marine Corps has a way of keeping its Marines moving from place to place, war to war. This means that after nearly 20 years of service a Marine who loves to fish can expect to have fished in quite a few places around the globe.

Every time I moved to a new duty station—southern California, Europe, New Hampshire, Hawaii, the Carolinas—or visited a place for a while—Japan, Florida, Virginia, the Middle East, Colorado—I would have to learn about the fish there in a hit-or-miss manner. I would start asking anglers what I should do when, where, and how. Book stores usually offered either a general treatise on fishing in a certain region, or a volume or two that covered only certain aspects of fishing thereabouts. This was especially true when it came to saltwater fishing.

I found this to be the situation when I arrived in the Carolinas as well. There was no book that effectively covered all aspects of inshore fishing the Carolinas' coasts. One book covered surf fishing, another surf, jetty, and pier techniques. Still another touched on trolling and other boat-related methods. Frustrating.

So I was once again required to start from scratch in the usual way. I asked every angler willing to talk to tell me about the fish he or she was after. I spoke with party or "head" boat captains, charter boat captains, guides, fellow outdoors writers, tournament specialists, bait and tackle shop owners, pier operators, and anybody else I could corner and coerce into parting with some advice. I fished every second I could in every likely looking spot I could get at. And I began to catch fish.

Lots of fish.

So this book. No longer will an angler new to Carolina waters have to cast in the dark for tidbits of information that may or may not pan out. This book covers it all.

For ease of use, the book is set up first by chapters covering individual species of game fish. The life history of each is discussed first, then tactics (including lure, bait, and tackle advice, as well as seasonal information), and finally hot spots such as where in the surf, river, sound, or lagoon you should focus your efforts for that particular species.

After the species chapters you will come to method chapters, each covering a different venue. For instance, you will read about how to: buy and set up the best types of inshore boats; work a pier like a pro; get far up a creek and take big fish from small holes; survey a beach to find the best spot for reds; anchor in a cut beside a rock jetty to fight flounder; wade a flat for drum; fish from a bridge for thick-bodied sheepshead; troll a mile offshore for maniacal king mackerel; cast to a buoy for a bruiser cobia; throw a Got-Cha plug for a spanish mackerel in a river mouth; work the drop-offs and inlets of the Intracoastal Waterway; fly fish for a tremendous variety of game fish; and much, much more.

Then we'll turn to the many threats to our inshore waters and what anglers can do to save these precious resources. Finally, you can find other practical and helpful information, including regulations you'll need to know, lists of piers, boat ramps, marinas, boat dealers, tackle shops, guides and party boats.

So come along for a learning tour of the Carolinas' coasts.

And bring your net.

# Contents

# Chapter 1
# Spotted Seatrout

Every region of the United States has a handful of species of fish that have gained special favor with those who would catch them. Florida has tarpon, bonefish, a variety of snappers. Maine has landlocked salmon, bluefish, brook trout. California's favorites are yellowtails, calico bass, rainbow trout, albacore. Minnesota offers walleye, northern pike, smallmouth bass. Massachusetts anglers are fond of cod, Atlantic mackerel, and fluke. In Missouri anglers enjoy brown trout, catfish, and crappie. Along the coasts of the Carolinas, the spotted seatrout, also known as a speck, or simply trout, is one of those special fish. It entices anglers from afar.

## Life History

The spotted seatrout's way of life is no great mystery, as the fish has been studied in depth largely because of its popularity with anglers and importance as a commercial species. Spawning takes place from early spring well into November, and occurs in the shallow bays and lagoons that decorate our coastline like opaque jewels. After the eggs hatch, the young fish and older juveniles move into shallow waters with substantial weed and grass growth. Here they will stay until winter, feeding on crustaceans and other tiny forms of marine life. Young trout are never far from the protection and sustenance offered by the shallows and their resident marine flora. As the waters grow cold with the fleeting autumn, the youngsters head into deeper waters to winter in the upper reaches of rivers and creeks where deep holes abound. A smaller percentage will leave the grassy lagoons for the pockets outside of the surf zone.

**A typical stringer of Carolina specks from the Atlantic Intracoastal Waterway.**

In the spring when the spawning run commences, seatrout school and begin foraging heavily. They come out of the holes in the upper reaches of coastal rivers where the water is brackish to pursue shrimp (edible, sand, snapping, and grass) in the rivers, as well as finger mullet, mummichogs (common killifish), glass minnows, and the young of various other fish. As summer approaches many of the specks will take up residence at the mouths of the rivers and creeks to gorge themselves on the rich marine life found in these zones. Autumn sees heavy schooling activity as in the spring, and the seatrout will once again begin their slow migration to brackish water and the outer surf zone. They regularly use the Atlantic Intracoastal Waterway to get from the mouth of one river to the upper end of a nearby river.

# Seatrout Tactics

With specks taking up living quarters from the surf and river mouths all the way up rivers and creeks to the freshwater mark, you might expect that tactics and techniques for catching these scrappers would run a wide gamut. And you would be 100 per cent correct! There are more ways to catch spotted seatrout along the Carolinas' coasts than you can shake a spinning rod at, and what follows are most of them. I say most because no matter where a trout bum goes, and no matter how many years he or she has been fishing for these rascals, there always seems to be a new approach to be discovered once there. Sometimes these techniques are found by just watching other anglers. Sometimes a bait and tackle shop owner will tell you a local secret that puts you onto the fish. And once in a great while another angler you don't know will part with some seatrout wisdom, although such events are comparatively rare due to the trout angler's tendency to be tight-lipped when it comes to hot locations and techniques.

## Soft-Bodied Jigs

With the advent of the soft-bodied jig more anglers began catching more seatrout. There are many makes and models out there on the market nowadays, and just about every angler has a favorite, so what strikes one person's fancy as being "the best" might not appeal to the next angler. Still, some favorite brands include Mister Twisters, Trout Magic, and my personal favorite, Sea Striker's Got-Cha curltails.

**Soft-bodied jigs for trout vary in color, design and size.**

There are three basic designs of soft-bodied jigs: grubs, which have fat bodies and a paddlelike tail; tube tails, which have thinner bodies dressed with stripped tails; and curled tails, which have a tail that curls or twists back up over the often ribbed body. More spotted seatrout are taken on curltails than the grubs or tubes, with the grubs being more productive and popular than the tubes. The reason for the curltails popularity and proven effectiveness on finicky trout is simple: the very flexible tail makes for a more lifelike action under a variety of conditions. Even with only a slight twitch of the rod tip the

3

curltail jig comes alive and tells a passing seatrout that dinner is nigh. Grubs sporting paddletails require a more vigorous action with the rod tip. Tubetails don't need much coaxing to get the stripped tails to move, but the action is still much more subtle than that of the curltail.

Soft-bodied jigs come in an intimidating array of colors and color combinations. However, seatrout prefer only about half a dozen of these. Chartreuse/silver flake, green/silver flake, smoke/silver flake, rootbeer, white/firetail, and lime green/silver flake are all known to be highly productive. There is no real need to have hundreds of jigs with you in two dozen color schemes. Carry these six patterns and you will have what you need almost all of the time.

For the average spotted seatrout cruising in the waters of North or South Carolina, a 4-inch jig is the appropriate size. But when you are after the equivalent of Florida's "gator" trout, meaning specks in the 10-pound range, you should switch to 6-inch jigs.

Two additional body designs that you sometimes see being thrown for seatrout are the doubletail and shrimptail. Although these two designs are known to catch seatrout from time to time, they do not compare with the curltail or paddletail. I keep only one or two with me when after specks just in case.

The color of the lead head you use with these jigs is very important. I have seen many a seatrout angler go home with only a grimace while others were fighting trout after trout because they had the right jig and head combination. Fluorescent orange and bright red heads are at the top of the hit parade. When you match a chartreuse/silver flake 4-inch curltail jig with a fluorescent orange head, you stand a pretty good chance of convincing a speck that what it is seeing is something good to eat. I usually start with this color combination, but keep a close eye on what other anglers are using. On many occasions I have had to make a quick switch to green or dark green with an orange or red head, or perhaps smoke/silver flake with an orange or red head when the chartreuse/silver flake didn't pan out. Specks will often insist on one particular color of jig and ignore everything else.

There are three basic lead head shapes used with soft-bodied jigs. Grub heads are the most popular and sport an eye. Trout heads are shorter and have no eye, and bullet heads are primarily used with doubletail jigs. Always have 1/4-, 3/8-, and 1/2-ounce heads with you to deal with varying current conditions, depths, and wind. Seatrout are fast-current fanatics, preferring channels and holes where the current really kicks up a fuss. Too light a lead head will make it difficult to get your jig down to the bottom so that it can be

**Dennis Adams works the waterway for gator trout.**

worked through the entire hole or along the complete length of the channel lip, trough, or oyster bar.

Ask two trouters how the body of the jig should go on the lead head—tail curled up or tail curled down, and you will probably get two different answers. I question whether it makes any difference. Still, out of habit more than anything, I put mine on tailed curled down. Arguments can be made supporting both methods.

## Hard-Bodied Jigs

There are still some die-hard seatrout nuts out there who prefer the old style hard-bodied (lead) jig or bucktail dressed with thin strands of nylon. They may know what they are doing, because these old-fashioned lures catch loads of trout. There are many head shapes available, too, and lately these anglers have taken to dressing the jig further with short plastic worms. This trick came about by watching bass anglers use similar worms on the end of their bass jigs. What works for bass, in this case, works for seatrout.

Colors good with soft-bodied jigs will do the same with bucktails. You can mix and match the worm trailer colors with the skirt dressing, too. As with the soft-bodies jigs, seatrout will often focus on one or two color patterns and pay no attention to others. Half-ounce and 5/8-ounce bucktails account for most of the seatrout taken on this design.

Now that different jig designs are out of the way, we need to look at how to use them. Seatrout are notoriously picky, and this characteristic doesn't apply only to colors. How you present the jig to the speck is just as important.

5

**The author with a fair catch of specks all taken on jigs.**

First we have the *lift and drop*. Cast out into a likely looking spot and allow the jig to drop all the way to the bottom. Slowly lift the rod tip about a foot and then quickly drop it. As the jig falls back to the bottom a seatrout will grab it. It doesn't inhale it the way a bass often does. Rather, it will take the jig into the forward part of its mouth and then turn to swim away. This is when the angler feels the "bump" or "tap" that says a trout is there. Seatrout will not often hold onto a jig very long at all, so a quick strike is needed, but only one strike: do not reset the hook. Spotted seatrout have soft mouths that tear easily, meaning that a second setting of the hook will often result in a lost fish. You won't need to set the hook a second time if your hooks are sufficiently sharp.

A tempting variation of this technique is to lift the rod tip quickly—snap it up—and then lower the rod tip (fast or slow). Watch and feel for the trout as it grabs the jig. The two ways most anglers lose seatrout are that they fail to set the hook fast enough and try to set the hook a second time because they think the first wasn't quite good enough.

The *crawl* is another excellent presentation. I first saw this demonstrated by an angler called Jesse and his buddy, The Colonel, in the Atlantic Intracoastal Waterway behind Onslow Beach. Jesse and The Colonel are local experts who use the crawl method regularly, and they regularly take stringers full of seatrout home at the end of the tide, too. With the rod tip pointing

**Trout action at Brown's Inlet during the fall run.**

slightly above level, reel the jig in *slowwwwly* along the bottom with an occasional pause. Trout swim up behind the jig and grab it as it begins to crawl again after a short stop.

The *triple scoot* is a presentation that can make a trout stop in its watery tracks and attack. Three quick jerks of the rod tip in succession made horizontal to the water's surface make the seatrout think that something is trying to get away in a hurry. The fish's instinctive strike reaction does it in.

Next is the *dead drift*. By allowing your jig just to tumble along the bottom with a strong current or running tide you can fool a trout into thinking that a dead bait fish is being swept past it. When all else fails, try this tactic.

Finally we have the *swim*. Cast the jig out and swim it in steadily just off of the bottom. The curltail jig is best for this method since the tail wiggles nicely and brings trout in for a look-see.

Before we move on to different lures, it may be very well worth your while to try a tandem jig rig. Two jigs 6 to 8 inches apart worked together sometimes convince even the wariest seatrout. Also, liquid fish attractants work very well on jigs. When fish smell odors their feeding instinct becomes sharper. A jig that has had a fish attractant like Baitmate shad or saltwater applied to it will get more attention. Trout tend to hang onto a jig, especially a soft-bodied jig longer if it has been treated with a liquid attractant. Yes, there are anglers out there who say that such products are a gimmick, but science and personal experience say they are wrong. A good fish attractant will get more fish on the hook. It's as simple as that.

7

**Having a good selection of jigs is important when the trout are being picky.**

## Hard-Sided Lures and Crankbaits

The only thing more numerous than types of soft- and hard-bodied jigs are hard-sided lures and crankbaits. There are literally hundreds of such lures decorating the shelves of bait and tackle shops along the Carolinas' coasts, and sometimes the toughest thing for a beginner trout angler to do is figure out which to buy. I'll attempt to narrow it down some so that you don't spend your life savings on lures.

Without a doubt the most famous spotted seatrout lures are MirrOlures. These outstanding lures have been around for many years, and every experienced seatrout angler has a selection in his tackle box. They come in a plethora of colors and patterns to handle most, if not all, situations. Floating

**MirrOlures have been taking seatrout for decades.**

models are great in the shallows and over oyster beds. Sinking models bumped along the bottom or through structure will bring strikes when other lures come up short. There are lipped models, too, that dive deep and have an action all their own. Popular colors include silver, silver with black spots, chartreuse and orange, white with a red head, and pink.

Bill Lewis Lures makes the renowned Rat-L-Trap series of classic bass crankbaits. Here is another example of a lure that has successfully crossed over to the seatrout venue. New models of these rattling lures have gained favor with seatrout anglers working all sorts of situations. The floating Rat-L-Trap in chartreuse shiner, gold, silver Tennessee shad, and chrome black back are known to drive big trout crazy. Spark-L-Traps in silverado, chartreuse blue, and west point special; the new saltwater version Mag-Trap in gold/hot pink and White Red Head/Dots; and the Slap-Stik in chartreuse shiner, chrome blue/black, and gold orange belly. The Slap-Stik is particularly effective in narrow channels in shallow, grassy lagoons.

Other top offerings for seatrout include: the Smithwick Rattlin' Rogue in black and chartreuse coach dog, gold with black back, and yellow chrome-green back; Bomber Long "A" minnow in silver flash/white back/red head, pearl/black to gray back/orange belly, and chartreuse flash/blue back/orange belly; Bomber BM7 Mullet in silver/red head/white, silver/black/white, and gold/green/white; Mann's Stretch 1-Minus in chartreuse, Tennessee shad, green shad chartreuse, and grey ghost; Rapala Shad Rap in silver fluorescent chartreuse and the Rapala original floating model in silver and silver fluorescent chartreuse.

Retrieving these lures can be broken down into three different methods. The *pull and pause* is used in heavy current and simulates a bait fish that is fighting the current and resting intermittently. Start with a steady retrieve and then dash it forward with either an increase in reeling speed or a long twitch of the rod tip. The *bottom bump* is used for diving models that can be twitched along the bottom stirring up debris. And the *steady* is simply retrieving the lure with no pauses or additional twitches of the rod tip.

## Live and Cut Bait

Few seasoned trout anglers would disagree with the statement that more big seatrout are taken on lively live shrimp than any other bait or lure. The fact is, spotted seatrout rely heavily on the shrimp population for their survival. In years when shrimp populations are low, seatrout catches also fall off. Most angling communities have a handful of specialists who have made names for themselves as anglers who catch lots of big trout. These professional trout

**Finger mullet are an important part of the speck's diet.**

anglers stick almost exclusively to large, fresh, lively shrimp, which they catch in cast nets, or buy from local bait shops when the shrimp are unavailable in the shallows.

Next to live shrimp, the seatrout likes "finger" mullet, which are in fact white mullet. They are known as finger mullet for their length, which is often about that of an adult man's middle finger. Like shrimp, finger mullet are often found in large numbers in the estuaries, creeks, and lagoons. They are especially plentiful in the surf, where they can be seen in huge schools that turn the water black.

Mummichogs, glass minnows, needlefish, small lizardfish and peeler crabs are also acceptable baits, but they are not nearly so often taken by seatrout as are shrimp and mullet.

**A simple live bait rig is made with an egg sinker, barrel swivel, and hook.**

Cut bait such as squid and mullet will sometimes coax a cruising seatrout. However, most taken in this manner are incidental catches. Drum anglers sometimes drag in a thrashing seatrout—which is a member of the drum/

10

croaker family—that happened by and liked the looks and smell of the squid or cut mullet on their hooks.

# Hot Spots

There is much more to angling for spotted seatrout than just knowing what to use and how to use it. All the lures, baits, and advice in the world would be of little use to the angler who doesn't know *where* to fish.

## In Surf

Winter trout that don't head up the creeks can be caught in holes just outside the surf zone. Look for breaks in the surf line and calm spots among otherwise raucous waters. The edges of rip tides are also likely hot spots.

**George Misko lets fly in the surf. The surf at his feet is filled with finger mullet.**

## In Rivers

Summer means trout in the mouths of rivers and creeks, as well as in very deep holes upriver. Jigs bounced in eddies and through troughs where the current is running strong, or a live shrimp fished on the bottom with a pyramid sinker that will hold in place are apt to land trout.

## In The Intracoastal Waterway

Spring and fall find specks moving *en masse* in the Intracoastal. Curltail jigs, live finger mullet, and live shrimp are all solid choices along channel drop-offs and near bridges. Also, hit the inlet mouths where they join with the

Waterway. Creek and estuary confluences are places you should never pass up, as are oyster beds with shallow water on one side and a deep trough on the other.

**Fishing vests are perfect for wading after trout.**

### In Lagoons And Backwaters

Quiet lagoons and backwaters with narrow slits for channels and sudden drop-offs where rivers cut through them are trout havens. If you see bait fish moving in the area, try one of the aforementioned crankbaits, especially Rat-L-Traps and Bomber BM 7 Mullets. As always, a live shrimp is pretty much a sure bet.

### From Piers

Anglers don't normally go looking for seatrout from piers. Most specks caught from piers are taken as incidentals by drum and flounder anglers. If you are on a pier, however, keep a live finger mullet running around among the pilings in case a trout comes along.

## Spotted Seatrout Tackle

Spotted seatrout tackle is readily available in most tackle and discount department stores. You don't need a $500 rod and an equally expensive reel.

### Rods

One need not buy a bunch of different trout rods. One wisely chosen rod will serve well in most situations. You will see new or unknowing seatrout anglers using rods that are much too heavy or much too light. Go with a fast or ultrafast action spinning rod between 6 1/2 and 7 feet long that handles 6-

to 10-pound test line. (I use a Shimano Black Aero, but there are many other good makes and models available.) For added fun, try a 5 1/2- or 6-foot ultralight rod.

## Reels

The same spinning reels you use for bass, catfish, and big crappie will suffice for trout. Fight the urge to go heavier than necessary, even when after gator trout. Even the largest trout doesn't run with your drag for long distances, and the fight normally lasts less than three minutes.

## Lines

Spotted seatrout have two canine teeth that can shred a line in short order. The new braided lines are outstanding for specks because their abrasion resistance can fend off these teeth as well as the hazards of oyster beds and barnacle-encrusted pilings. There is no need to go any heavier than 12-pound test.

# Weakfish or Gray Trout

The spotted seatrout's first cousin, the weakfish, known along the Carolinas' coasts as the gray trout, looks similar to a speck but lacks the well-defined black spots along the back and tail, and has yellowish fins. It inhabits the same waters as the speck, eats the same foods, spawns in the same areas, schools like a speck, pretty much fights likes a speck, and tastes like a speck.

So it must be a speck, right? Wrong. It really is a completely different fish.

Actually, there are a few differences when compared to habits and habitat. The grays will go farther north than specks and well out into deeper water come winter.

Many anglers believe that the gray fights better than the speck, since they are prone to making pretty impressive initial runs and throwing in a sudden, unexpected turn now and then. And grays are more likely to be lured in by a chum line. So you can catch many a gray trout right in the same waters as a speck, on the same bait or lure, and on the same rod and reel.

I see no need to have a separate chapter on the gray trout because the two are so close. Spotted seatrout come in schools; they often weigh five pounds or more (although three and four pounders are much more common); they put up a good fight, and they make good table fare to boot. Is it any wonder that they have earned a spot in the hearts of countless anglers?

# Chapter 2
# Bluefish

Few fish out of the 25,000 or so species in existence today can be considered to have a "bad reputation." Fewer still can be thought of as world class game fish. The bluefish is one of these few.

The bluefish has been notorious for centuries. Drawings from ancient Greece depict bluefish and their nasty teeth, as do drawings made by Native Americans. Colonists here were taught early on about the fish that slices fingers with one quick snap of a powerful jaw. All new bluefish anglers are first taught to respect the fish's ability (and apparent strong desire!) to chew up human hands, or for that matter anything else that gets near its mouth.

As a fighter the bluefish has only a handful of equals, among them the permit, bonefish, Atlantic salmon, yellowtail, and snook. When a blue attacks its quarry, carnage and mayhem result. It doesn't just eat: it feasts. On the hook it goes wild with anger, sounding, jumping, thrashing, and stripping line in the same manner that it tears through a school of menhaden. It will allow itself to be brought close to the boat, and then streak off toward the horizon with the helpless angler's reel seeming to smoke as line peels off the spool at an astonishing rate.

Blues have been known to attack humans as well, but all of these assaults are thought to be the result of mistaken identity. When blues begin to feed in choppy, murky water, and there is a surfeit of bait in the water, a veritable feeding frenzy often results. The rampaging blues careen wildly through the fleeing, terrified bait fish, which have been known to jump onto shore to escape the maniacal predators chasing them to their doom. Bathers standing or swimming in such a madhouse have had fingers, hands, arms, toes, legs, and even torsos bitten badly in the melee. In some cases dozens of stitches have been required.

Bluefish are found from Argentina at the tip of South America to the Canadian Maritimes in the western Atlantic Ocean, and offer the finest in sport fishing. Carolina blues invade the inshore waters in the spring and can be caught well into autumn, and in some years into early winter. However, once the waters turn cold, they head for warmer climes.

# Life History

Bluefish often spawn over rocky bottoms in the shallows, usually in 10 feet of water or less. Shallows that have a ledge facing open water are preferred to broad flats protected from the open sea by land features. Some blues do not venture close to shore and stay out at sea to procreate. A single female will be attended by a few males, and as the female turns on one side to discharge her eggs, the males rush in and fertilize them. The eggs are free floating, and the resulting larvae drift with the currents as well.

The growth rate of blues is phenomenal in the first year. Newly hatched fish eat voraciously as soon as they can. Known as snappers, these tiny bluefish can easily grow to a foot or more in length in the first year. Average growth per year is about a pound and a half, but faster rates have been noted in areas where bait fish are especially prolific.

At about age six, the blue's growth rate begins to level off, but they don't stop growing. The late A.J. McClane, author of *McClane's Standard Fishing Encyclopedia* and *McClane's Field Guide to Saltwater Fishes of North America*, and fishing editor at *Field & Stream* magazine, noted that a 45-pound bluefish was taken off the coast of North Africa, but the International Game Fish Association states that the all-tackle record weighed 31 pounds, 12 ounces and was caught by James M. Hussey on January 30, 1972, off Cape Hatteras. (Note that the world record was taken in the dead of winter.)

It is unusual to catch bluefish of radically differing sizes from the same school. This is because blues are cannibals that will not hesitate to eat smaller versions of themselves if the opportunity presents itself. Young blues will be packed tightly into a school, while the larger they get the more room they leave between each other. It seems that after a bluefish hits the 15-pound mark the number in a school will drop off dramatically. Twenty-pound blues operate in schools of four to six, and bigger ones may not school at all.

As is the case with many species of fish, bluefish populations will occasionally "crash" for no apparent reason. Biologists believe that this may be due to sudden depletions of forage fish such as menhaden and mullet, which feed on tiny crustaceans, plankton, and shrimp larvae. When plankton levels drop, so do the number of menhaden. This chain reaction may effect the bluefish populations in turn.

Bluefish migrate not only from south to north with the warming weather and water, but from east to west. The Carolinas see outstanding bluefishing starting in April, and depending on the number of finger mullet in the area these fish will stay around and continue to feed heavily until June. Blues can still be caught all summer long, but the good fishing doesn't start up again until autumn when the bluefish begin making their run back down the coast. The huge schools of blues that run from 10 to 15 pounds and haunt the coast of Maine from July to autumn do not leave that area until late September or early October and usually don't show up in Carolina waters until late October or November, but their arrival is the highlight of the year for bluefish anglers.

**Chief Kevin Garner of the Royal Navy with a hefty bluefish taken on a Storm Big Mac.**

# Bluefish Tactics

Although bluefish are known for vicious appetites and eat a wide variety of food—everything from mackerel and menhaden to mullet and mummichogs—they can be selective at times. The right lure or bait is at times crucial to the bluefisher's success. But no matter what you troll or cast for blues, it must be *rugged* if you want to use it the next time you go fishing. Metal and tough plastic lures are required in this sport. Wooden plugs that your grandfather gave you should not be thrown at bluefish unless you are trying to get rid of them.

## Trolling Lures

One of the most enjoyable methods of catching bluefish is to troll large, lipped lures. These should be trolled fast, because the fish that flee before the chomping blues aren't wasting any time getting out of their way. A bluefish expects its prey to be moving *fast*. I have found that speeds between four and six knots are not too fast for bluefish, and if you are trolling a favorite lure with minimal results, you should consider increasing your speed before changing your bait or location.

Since you are going to be trolling at a fast clip, be sure to check the action of your lure at boat side before letting it go aft. Some lures that function as designed at three knots lose that ability at four knots or greater. They'll spin wildly or just drag themselves across the surface.

Storm's Big Mac series is an outstanding trolling lure. My favorite is a gold and orange model that I found attached to a lobster pot line. I suspect its previous owner was rather irritated at losing it, because it has been a real blue getter for me. No doubt it was for him as well. Rapala Magnums and Slivers are also super trolling lures for big blues. Like the Storm Big Mac, they function well at a quick pace. Gold fluorescent red, silver mackerel, and plain silver are colors you will want to have in Rapala Magnums, and gold fluorescent red, needlefish, and silver fluorescent chartreuse in the Rapala Slivers. Sizes should range from 5 1/2 to 7 inches in the Magnums, and 5 1/4 to 8 inches in the Slivers.

Mann's Stretch Depth Plus series offers contenders, too. Gray ghost, fire red fluorescent, and golden sunset patterns all take blues, and they come in three different models that cover the water column from 10 to more than 25 feet. When the blues are close to the surface, 7-inch Rebel Minnows in green mackerel and silver blue have proven their worth, as have Rebel Spoonbill and Fastrac Minnows of similar lengths. Spoonbill patterns should include gold/black, silver/green, and silver/red back, while the Fastracs should be in gold/orange back, green mackerel, gold/black, and Tennessee shad.

Mag-Traps in hot pink, gold chartreuse, and chrome chartreuse have recently become popular. The floating model of this lure is a knock-out over shallow bars and in calm surf.

Spoons seem to have a magical effect on hungry blues. I took my first bluefish on a big Krocodile spoon. After a fight that I fully expected to lose,

**Sunrise often means fast action for spring and fall blues.**

the awesome fish suddenly decided that he had had enough and came along-side. My partner, John Shesler, gaffed the fish and hauled him into the boat, where the fight began all over again. Three spoons you should keep in your tackle box are the Hopkins, Kastmaster, and the Krocodile in various sizes; some with tail dressing, others without.

The folks at Rebel are not often thought of as designers of trolling spoons, but they have come up with two winners: the South Port Slammer and Arrowhead trolling spoons. The silver models are what you want for bluefish.

Trolling for blues involves much more than just wandering around in your boat dragging a lure behind you. Blues are often found cruising at certain depths, and if you don't get your lure down to that depth, and you don't run it at the right speed, you will be far less successful than those anglers who know how to find the fish. A fish/depth finder and downrigger combination is a system that the best bluefish anglers have on their boats and know how to use well. Once you learn the simple science of fish/depth finder and downrigger use, you must master the art of knowing in which areas to start your search. Although the surface may look the same everywhere, it's what's on the bottom that makes the difference in most cases.

Nautical charts will show the reefs, ledges, and other anomalies that hold the schools of bait fish the blues hunt. Find these spots, and find blues. Also, river mouths and the outer surf zones are both good places to begin your quest.

**Birds working the surface mean bait and game fish are there.**

Watch the horizon for bird activity, and keep an eye on the surface for slicks of menhaden oil. Atlantic menhaden are an important forage fish for blues and are very oily. When a school is chewed up by a pack of bluefish, the oil and chunks of menhaden float on or near the surface. This is a sure sign of bluefish in the area.

This brings us to how a school of bluefish goes about feeding on a school of hapless forage fish. A school of blues will charge through a school of victims chomping at them in order to wound or outright kill them. They are not often eating during this time, just killing and maiming. When the bait fish—or what is left of the bait fish—disburse, the blues circle back and begin feeding on the dead and dying fish.

## Surf Plugs

Fighting an enraged blue in the crashing surf is exciting beyond description. The combination of a wild fish trying its hardest to empty your reel of line while salt spray and waves pummel you in chest deep water makes for long-term memories that never diminish.

Many of the trolling lures mentioned for blues will also work in the surf. But for excitement that will make blood course through your veins, try a surface plug.

Heddon's Zara Spook, the Creek Chub Striper Strike, and any pencil popper worked aggressively along the surface so that loud splashes and chugs cause a commotion will drive blues into fits of anger. A bluefish attacking a surface plug is a sight to see, with the water boiling, birds diving in the surf for wounded bait fish, blood in the water, and anglers all hollering encouragement to each other as the fracas grows happily wilder.

Some experienced anglers claim that they can "smell" or "sniff out" a school of blues. What they are smelling isn't bluefish but a phytoplankton bloom. It is merely a coincidence that blues are there when they smell this aroma wafting down the beach.

**A school of finger mullet negotiates the Carolina surf.**

## Live and Cut Bait

Few methods of catching bluefish are as thrilling as using live bait, or as productive. There are few things in life that can compare to live-lining a nervous "pogy" in an area where bluefish are prowling.

But before you can use live bait, you have to get live bait. In most instances this is quite a simple task. Menhaden (pogies, mossbunkers) are best caught by a weighted treble hook, shock or "shorty" wire leader, and a stout spinning rod. Cast the hook into a school of passing pogies and set the hook hard when you feel the hook bump into one. Reel it in and drop it in the live well. Half an hour in a decent school of pogies will produce dozens of fish. The shock or shorty wire leader is needed in case a bluefish decides to hit the pogy you are reeling in.

Finger mullet can be caught by the hundreds right off the beach. A cast net is all you need. You'll see them coming down the beach as a dark mass or a length of rippled water. Watch the face of the waves when they crest, then throw the net.

There are several ways to hook and fish live bait. One of the most effective is a split tandem rig I designed one morning while fishing for hefty blues with John Shesler. We were back hooking pogies and catching the occasional blue,

21

**George Misko shows how you are supposed to throw a cast net.**

**One throw of the net can mean easy pickings for bait.**

but most of the time the pogy was simply being bitten in half or had its tail chopped off. The solution was the Newman bluefish rig.

At the terminal end of a 24-inch, 30-pound test steel leader attach two shorty (6-inch) 15-pound test leaders, one with a stainless steel size 5/0 treble hook, the other with a stainless steel size 4/0 knife-edge point Mustad-Sea Hawk. Nose hook the pogy (open mouthed) with the single hook, and back

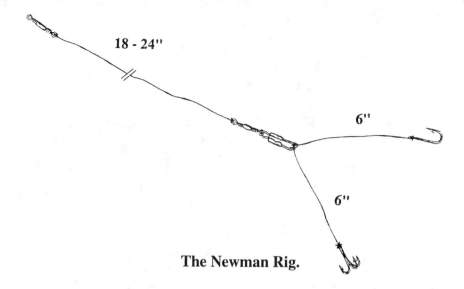

**The Newman Rig.**

hook it with the treble hook a couple of inches before the tail. This "stinger" system will greatly increase the number of blues caught.

Live bait fishing is usually done from a boat while anchored or drifting. Cast the bait out and let it swim around on its own with the bail open or the reel on free spool. (Shimano's Baitrunner reels are outstanding for this technique; the Model 6500 is best.) You'll be able to tell when the bait has been spotted by a bluefish because it will start swimming rapidly and erratically in an attempt to escape. When the blue hits, the line will either go slack—if the blue hit and killed the fish—or suddenly go very tight—the blue has taken the whole fish. If the line goes slack, close the bail (or take the reel off free spool), and wait for the blue to take the dead or dying bait. When the line suddenly tightens again, lean into the fish and set the hook hard. If the blue takes the bait right off the bat, lean into it as best you can and then set the hook. If you miss it, *do not* reel in right away. Instead, wait for a few moments to see if it comes back or another fish takes it.

Cut bait can be used with excellent results both during and after a frenzy, and even when no heavy feeding activity is apparent. Mini-steaks, belly-to-belly fillets, and whole tails cut from bait fish and rigged as rotation baits all attract blues. Squid and eel chunks will work as well. In fact, just about any type of bait will be hit if a frenzy is taking place, and there will be no doubt when this is occurring. The water will boil and erupt with fleeing bait fish and charging bluefish. Gulls, terns, and pelicans will all show up, and other anglers will seem to come from all directions. Few events in sport fishing are as exciting and awe inspiring as a bluefish feeding frenzy.

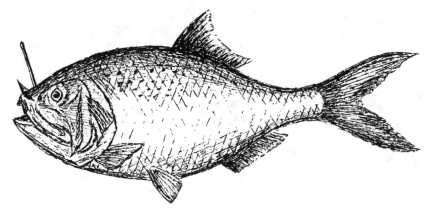

**Nose hook.**

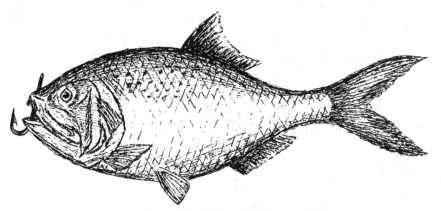

**Nose hook/double-lip.**

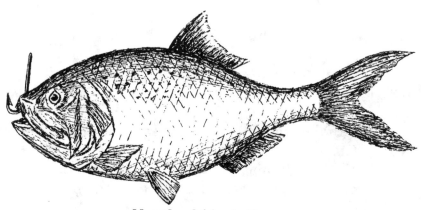

**Nose hook/single-lip.**

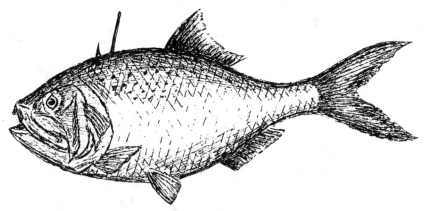

**Back hook/forward.**

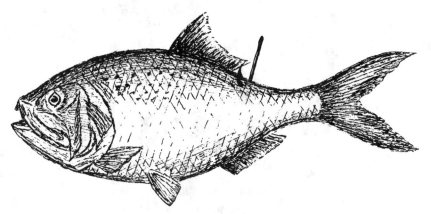

**Back hook/rear.**

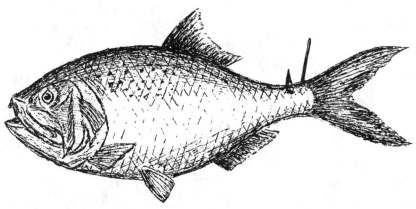

**Tail hook.**

# Hot Spots

Blues can be caught in many more areas other than the aforementioned. They may stay in a particular spot for a few hours, or even a few days, and there is no way to tell how long they will remain.

**Two finger mullet rigged above a pyramid sinker is an excellent bluefish rig for the beach.**

## In The Surf

Rocks and holes in the surf, either on the outside edge or right in the middle of the zone, are places to start trying. Fish the edges of rip tides and along rock jetties. Blues don't mind rough water, so don't hesitate to cast into tumultuous areas.

## In Rivers

Bluefish sometimes prowl rivers right to the fresh-water mark if they are chasing schools of bait fish. Otherwise, they will stay toward the mouth or only go upriver until fresh water drives them back. Wherever the bait is, the bluefish will be, too. They are not shy about going into shallows, and a good place to drift a live menhaden is where the shallows meet the channel. Anchor or wade into the shallows and cast out over the ledge.

## In Lagoons And Backwaters

As the spring and fall seasons begin to wane, check the lagoons and backwaters for tardy blues. Such spots are frequently productive when other more commonly fished areas are no longer hot. Oyster and mussel beds frequently are good spots.

**Blues are frequently caught right at the pier's end.**

## From Piers

Bluefish action around piers can be fast and furious. Got-Cha plugs tossed into schools of spanish mackerel or sea mullet will often be hit by a prowling bluefish.

## Near Shore

Channel markers and buoys are likely spots for bluefish looking for an easy meal, but the best fishing from a boat is usually in the area within 100 yards of the surf zone. These areas often give up cobia, king, and spanish mackerel, too.

# Bluefish Tackle

With some species of game fish the angler can afford to make selections that are somewhat vague. But in the bluefish war, you had better choose your weapons carefully. Flimsy slow-action rods and spider web line are not what you want unless you are after an IGFA line-class record. On the other hand, you don't want to go too heavy. The best bluefish anglers know the happy median.

## Rods

There is no one "best" bluefish rod for all occasions. However, some can come pretty darn close to being fine all-around rods. For the big autumn blues in the surf, an 8- to 9-foot medium action surf rod designed for 12- to 20-pound test line is a good choice. I use a Lamiglas 8 1/2 footer for these conditions, which gives me great casting distance and fighting power with its extended butt. For trolling I prefer a 7-foot fast action rod that allows me to control the fish better near the boat. For schoolies ("snappers") and "choppers" in the rivers and off jetties I like a 6 1/2- or 7-foot rod, also fast action. These last two rods hold 8- to 10-pound test. Other rods lengths and actions are commonly used, but slow action rods, ultralight shorties in the 5-foot category, and telephone pole rods that require blinking lights on the tips so that planes do not run into them should be avoided. A rod too light or too heavy will only frustrate you.

## Reels

Spinning reels capable of holding a few hundred meters of line are the norm, along with levelwind trolling reels. Penn and Shimano make the best levelwinds, and Shimano, Abu-Garcia, and Daiwa make outstanding spinning reels.

The drag system is crucial on a spinning or trolling reel. You must have a rugged, smooth drag that doesn't skip or catch under extreme pressure. Star drags on levelwinds and rear drags on spinning reels that are easy to get to and adjust are preferred. You should have your drag set right before you make that first cast, because adjusting the drag during the fight is generally not a good idea: it is too easy to tighten or loosen it too much causing a lost fish. Only adjust your drag during a fight when you have no other choice because of an unexpectedly large or powerful fish.

## Line

Centuries ago, anglers in Europe used horsehair for fishing line. Silk came along later, followed by this, that, and the other thing. Monofilament came into its own in the '50s, and was partially replaced in the '80s with polyfilaments and cofilaments. Each of these improvements was a step in the right direction, but few were as important as the introduction of the new braided lines. Yes, they are expensive, and you may have to learn a new knot or two, but they last longer, are very rugged, and dependable under stress. These lines take abuse! In fact, one line manufacturer (DuPont) makes their braided line out of Kevlar, which is what the military uses to make its helmets and body armor (flak jackets). Braided lines have almost no stretch, which means more sensitivity and firmer hook sets.

The polyfilaments are still favored by most anglers because they are more affordable and are known to the anglers. Stren, Ande, and Trilene are all popular lines. When fishing for blues, you just can't afford to go with a cheap line that will part when the going gets ugly.

Line classes should run between 8- and 20-pound test, and there is no need to go any higher because you are going to be using a shock or steel wire leader.

A 30-pound test polyfilament or braided shock leader or a 15- to 30-pound test steel wire leader is standard fare. Use the shortest one you can get away with. I seldom go longer than 24 inches, and will use an 18-inch or 12-inch whenever I can. For snapper blues and light choppers I will try and use a 6-inch shorty at first.

## Hooks

Bronze and stainless steel are the two metals used for bluefish. Most other hooks run the risk of shattering or straightening under strain. The most commonly used are 2/0 to 4/0.

## Other Things

A sturdy gaff, hook removers (long shank), cotton glove (for grasping the blue by the tail if you intend to catch and release the fish), and bandages are miscellaneous items you should have along. A club is a good idea, too, so that the angry bluefish trashing your boat can be persuaded to calm down.

Bluefish are aquatic combatants with few equals. They are often found in great numbers, will smack all sorts of lures and bait, and will give it their all right up until the bitter end. They taste good, too, when prepared correctly.

# Chapter 3
# Red Drum

The red drum is a species of game fish that has turned what would normally be staid, carefree anglers into wild-eyed, surf-charging fanatics who live, breathe, and eat reds. Such ardor is brought about for one reason: the red drum, a.k.a. redfish, bullred, puppy drum, spottail bass, channel bass, and rat-red, fights with the mettle of an incensed Marine. Even the smaller puppy drum that go around 15 inches and two pounds will make a lightweight reel beg for mercy.

The red drum is closely related to the spotted seatrout, weakfish, white seabass, croaker, Atlantic kingfish, silver seatrout, jackknife-fish, and black drum. They are bottom feeders, commonly taking crustaceans, mollusks, and various bait fish. (The finger mullet is a definite favorite.) Found in the surf, channels, and estuaries, in the lagoons and on the flats, reds will readily inhale a number of lures and baits ranging from small spinnerbaits and surface plugs, to whole finger mullet and cut squid.

The smaller reds (puppy drum) are outstanding on the table, and are fabulous "blackened" with Cajun spices and flash fried. Larger ones are usually released partly because they are woody in taste and partly because they are so important for the continuation of the species.

# Life History

Red drum spawn in the fall in the near-shore waters of the sounds. The young are believed to hang in the lagoons and channels in grass flats and in estuaries. Along the Carolinas' coasts, populations are somewhat local, with migration taking place in the fall when the adults move from the channels into the estuaries, sounds, and creeks. Unlike its cousin the spotted seatrout, which, for the most part, goes upriver for the winter, drum head out to sea. In the spring the reds move back toward shore and take up residence in the surf, cuts, estuaries, creeks, and rivers, often venturing well into fresh water with no apparent ill effects.

Red drum sometimes migrate because of salinity, water temperature, and the fluctuations of forage. Along the Gulf coasts of Florida and Texas there are drum populations that are apparently permanent. No migration occurs, even during the spawning season.

Courtesy of DuPont Stren

**Puppy drum are great fun on light tackle.**

32

# Red Drum Tactics

Comparatively few red drum anglers know that reds will willingly hit all kinds of lures and baits. Surface plugs, crankbaits, soft-bodied jigs, hard-bodied jigs, lipped minnows, cut bait, bloodworms, live bait, streamer flies, crabs—just about anything that a drum thinks is food, it will eat. He's a scrounger and doesn't care who thinks bad of him because of it.

Except in the dead of winter, reds are available. They can be found from fresh water seaward, and can be caught under many conditions. They are regularly taken by anglers fishing for seatrout and flounder. With such a broad diet and ability to thrive under almost all conditions, tactics for drum are expectedly diverse.

**Paddletail, straighttail, curltail and shrimptail jigs are all taken by reds.**

## Soft-bodied Jigs

Red drum are different from their seatrout relatives in another way: they seem to like the paddletail grub and doubletail jig just as much as the curltail jig. Bounced, hopped, and skittered across the soft bottoms that reds feed on, rootbeer/silver flake, motoroil/gold flake, avocado, and clear/silver flake grubs and jigs with yellow, white, fluorescent, and maroon heads will draw strikes. Like the seatrout, reds have a highly developed sense of smell. A grub or jig doused with a liquid fish attractant produces positive results.

Although 4-inch curltails and 2-inch grubs take their share of redfish, it is a good idea to carry 6-inch doubletails and 4-inch grubs when the bigger reds are in. Tubetails also prove their worth on the redfish grounds, as do shrimptails. Motoroil and silver/firetail for both of these soft-bodied designs work well. A variation of the curltail, Mann's Augertail grub in shrimp, white fluorescent, avocado, amber, smoke, and green metal flake with various leadhead colors have a slightly different action than the standard curltail and sometimes get attention when others don't.

Mann's also makes the Swimmin' grub, which has a ribbed body and an odd looking tail that wags when retrieved, and the George-N-Shad, which is a soft crankbait and jig combination with a single treble hook. Pearl, clear/metal flake, Tennessee shad, and wild shiner are the colors best suited for reds.

You can coax cautious redfish on slow days by threading a bucktail worm onto a leadhead. Yellow, chartreuse, white and motoroil take their fair share.

An old trick that still works wonders, and which attests to the drums sense of smell, is to "tip" the jig's hook with a dead shrimp. The odor of the shrimp and the sight of a skeedattling jig tell redfish that dinner is served. If you don't have shrimp, try a thin strip of squid (or two or three squid legs), or an equally thin strip of flounder belly.

## Hard-bodied Jigs

Most reds taken on hard-bodied jigs are incidentals hooked by flounder and striper anglers working ledges beside flats. If you decide to try your luck with bucktails, soak the skirt well with an attractant to better the odds.

There is a style of hard-bodied jig that is more productive than the traditional bucktail, and that is the chenille jig. Crappie anglers know these light jigs are devastating on "slabs" and use them on reds as well. Chartreuse, yellow, white, and lime green are best.

## Spinnerbaits

On the flats, in the lagoons and channels, and up near fresh water (and right into fresh water) small spinnerbaits like the Beetlespin are known to be highly effective on puppy drum. The key to using spinnerbaits for these upriver reds is small size. Avoid the big, heavy spinnerbaits that bass anglers drag through stump fields and along weed lines for bucketmouth *hawgs*. The light Beetlespins in lime green and white, or Bomber Mini-Whackers in white, green, yellow, and chartreuse combination skirts with and without trailers are super redfish baits.

There are reams of spinnerbaits on the market today, with a mess of blade designs. Single Colorado blades are most effective, with willow blades coming in second.

Courtesy of Bill Lewis

**This red hit a Rat-L-Trap, one of the hottest lures around.**

## Crankbaits

Of all the lure types available to modern anglers, the crankbait must be the most diverse. There seems to be a new crankbait beckoning from the shelf of the local tackle shop every day. Where do you start?

With redfish it is fairly easy. Pick a crankbait that imitates a bait fish picking crustaceans off of the bottom or darting overhead, and you can catch redfish with it. Nevertheless, color does play a role.

35

I'll recommend some crankbaits that have done well for me and some of my cohorts, but the truth is that you may have luck with entirely different colors. Light and water conditions come into play, as do the predominant bait fish in the area at the time. If the finger mullet are in, try light colors. If the mummichogs are about, go with green. And so on.

Cotton Cordell Super Spots in super shad, Tennessee shad, chrome/black and chartreuse vibrate well in the water and that apparently turns redfish on. The Rebel Creek Creature in stream demon, mad tom blue, and phantom pink vibrates much like the Super Spot and dives deep. The Rat-L-Trap series gained favor rapidly once red specialists found out that drum will chase them under a variety of conditions. Lectric gold, fire tiger, gold/black back with orange belly, and orange crawdad are four excellent color schemes. Striper, chartreuse shad, bone/orange belly, and parrot also work. Rat-L-Traps all have tiny ball bearings inside them that make a racket when retrieved. Redfish orient on sound and vibrations as much as they do on odor under some conditions, which explains why noisy crankbaits are in vogue.

**Small Rapalas worked along the bottom or twitched on top are a good bet.**

More solid bets include the Bomber Model "A" in bright colors like orange, yellow, and chartreuse; Helen's famous flatfish in the same bright colors; the Lazy Ike in fire tiger, metallic blue, and yellow spot; ThinFins in light colors; Rapala Fat Raps in fire tiger and silver fluorescent chartreuse;

Rattlin' Rapalas in green shad, gold black, and fire tiger; and jointed and floating model Rapala minnows in silver, gold fluorescent red, and fire tiger.

I think it important here to say that these lures and color combinations are what I have found to turn redfish on. But I haven't fished every lure available. There are dozens, maybe hundreds of models that I have never tried, probably because what I have been using works and I see no reason to take chances with other lures. Then again, some I've never heard of no doubt will get a redfish's ire up.

## Surface Plugs

Redfish are very susceptible to surface plugs when they are in the shallows, and I have seen reds charge up off of the bottom 10 feet below to get at a plug on top. So "shallow" water is certainly relative. Plugging on the surface in redfish country is just as much fun as popping for smallmouth bass in northern Maine's Washington County and snook in Florida's mangrove swamps lining the southern Everglades. If only redfish jumped like those two species!

I believe that plugs irritate redfish. For some reason they strike surface lures angrily, much as a bluefish hits a big pencil popper in the middle of an assault on a school of pogies. The strike is downright *mean*. Some of the better surface plugs include the Smithwick Devil Horse in just about any color; the Nip-I-Diddee (a fat, torpedo-like lure with propellers on each end that first got anglers, attention in the Loxahatchee area of the Florida Everglades; Rat-L-Stiks; Zara Spooks; Rapala and Rebel floating minnows (twitched like a wounded bait fish rather than steadily cranked in); and Hula Poppers. Color appears to be of less importance when using surface plugs, with action and noise being what the reds are interested in.

## Spoons

Anglers hunting reds do not use spoons as much as they use live or cut bait and crankbaits, but spoons can be quite effective. Retrieved across channel and estuary mouths, and through lagoons, spoons like the Johnson silver minnow tipped with a piece of white pork rind, Swedish Pimple, Wob-L-Rite, Dardevle, Weeping Willow, and Mooselook Wobbler all imitate bait fish. Try them next time.

**Heavier drum work the surf, and this angler is in prime position along the beach at Surf City.**

**Carlos Briones works French Creek for autumn drum.**

## Live and Cut Bait

Live and cut bait probably take more redfish than all other types. This is so because of the nature of a redfish: it is a scrounger that uses its sense of smell to detect prey. Do not restrict yourself to the traditional live or cut mullet, however. Bloodworms, sandworms, clams, sandbugs, chunks of menhaden, live and dead shrimp, and crabs are all on the red drum's menu.

Carlos Briones, a red drum pro out of Jacksonville, N.C., prefers small (3-inch) finger mullet fished on a 1/0 Tru-Turn hook. Carlos goes as light as possible using 6-pound test line for puppy drum and a light rod. Split shot is used for weight rather than an egg or pyramid sinker, unless a strong tide is running. He is convinced that reds can detect heavier line and terminal gear, and has proved this by fishing a heavy setup with identical bait right beside a light setup on numerous occasions. The lighter setup always produces many more strikes. He also stresses the importance of going with a small finger mullet, not a big one.

Menhaden fillets and chunks (and any other cut bait) should be as fresh as possible. Drum will pass over old, stale bait. Change it frequently. Also, a flounder belly/squid combination, menhaden fillet/dead shrimp combination, and herring fillet/flounder belly combination will get a red drum to bite if the bait is fresh.

**Late fall action leaves room for plenty of anglers on the beach.**

# Hot Spots

Just as with bluefish, one day will offer fast action in one place, the next in another. But once you find a productive spot it will usually produce fairly steadily if you use the right bait and tackle.

## In The Surf

The surf is the classic red drum location. Reds cruise the beach searching for deep holes and sloughs right amongst the waves. As the outgoing tide begins to slow, red drum anglers can be seen patrolling the beach in their 4-wheel drive vehicles looking for these spots, the front of their trucks adorned

Courtesy of Daiwa

**Just right for the dinner table.**

with PVC pipe holding a selection of surf rods. They are watching the waves for plunging surf, which means the water there is deeper. They are watching for rips and rock piles, and cuts that channel water to and fro. The key is moving water that will bring food to the reds. Smooth water means less action because the reds will have to hunt more vigorously there. Points and spits with deep cuts on the side are perfect for big drum. The incoming tide is red drum time in such places.

## In Rivers, Creeks, And Estuaries

River mouths, inlets between barrier islands, feeder creeks, and coastal estuaries give up drum running anywhere from two to 20 pounds, and then some. However, most are in the single digits. Drop-offs and holes hold the best and most drum, and finding these hot spots is a matter of luck and know-how. By running your depth finder in a river you can easily plot holes, drop-offs, and troughs. Listen carefully to anglers conversing on the beach and in tackle shops: they may mention a hot spot you can fish.

## In Lagoons And Backwaters

Anglers can stalk small to medium red drum in shallow lagoons and on sand flats just as bonefish, permit, and tarpon anglers do in the Florida Keys and Bahamas. This is a sport all its own that has gained in popularity over the years and now has many proponents. Guides from Beaufort, S.C., to the Outer Banks who specialize in stalking reds in the shallows are partly responsible for this phenomenon, along with word-of-mouth advice and magazine articles espousing the fun and thrills found in fighting on light gear drum that you have hunted by sight.

Starting in late March and early April, waders quietly shuffle across lagoons and flats with small crankbaits, jigs, surface plugs, and even live shrimp on the end of their lines looking for clouds of sand or mud stirred up by foraging redfish. Sometimes you will see them "tailing" much like bonefish, and they sometimes come in schools. When you spot a school, don't cast into the middle of it because if you frighten one the others will flee as well. Cast well out to the side of the school and work the lure toward it.

## From Piers

Live and cut bait takes loads of reds from Carolina piers starting in the spring and lasting into June, then again in the fall. As is in fishing for blues, find a spot along the pier over a hole or cut, if you can, and lower a fresh chunk

**Drum are caught in the surf below most Carolina piers.**

of cut bait or a cut bait combination into it. Around piers you will need a stiffer rod and stouter line than in the surf because of the barnacles and oysters attached to the pilings: you must be able to control that redfish when you hook it.

### Near Shore

By anchoring outside the surf zone along a cut, rip, or trough you can position yourself over some of the hottest redfish action possible. When a long shore current is running, try drifting live finger mullet, mud minnows, or cut bait. As the boat passes through areas of calmer water, put the rod in a rod holder and tighten the drag in case a stray nails your bait while you are casting with another rod toward more productive looking holes and cuts. Watch for reds feeding along the bottom in the wave troughs.

# Red Drum Tackle

Red drum can attain weights of nearly 100 pounds. The IGFA all-tackle record is 94 pounds 2 ounces set by David G. Deuel on November 7, 1984,

**The author keeping an eye out for drum along Onslow Beach.**

at Avon, N.C. on the Outer Banks. With fish this size ready to gobble your bait you must make very sure you have the right tackle. The wrong gear can lead to disappointment.

## Rods

Where the giants of the species live off the Outer Banks, anglers working the beach in spring and fall go with powerful surf rods between 8 to 11 feet long. Some use fiberglass, while others have made the switch to graphite, which is generally stronger and always more sensitive than fiberglass. Graphite rods, especially long surf rods, used to be extremely expensive, but have become more affordable as manufacturing technology has advanced. Long rods serve two purposes: they have the backbone to get a lot of weight (sinkers and big baits) out to the holes and sloughs, and they can handle huge redfish that have no intention of willingly going to the beach. A 50-pound bull is not a fish that can be toyed with, and it will wreck a light rod in a heartbeat.

For smaller river and inlet drum, a 6- to 7-foot medium or medium light rod, fast action, is fine. I have used a Daiwa ultralight (5 1/2-foot) to wrestle drum in the Intracoastal, but handling these sluggers on such a rod is very difficult, although it can be done.

## Reels

Reels with deep spools that hold plenty of line are vital. Shallow spools will be emptied in a matter of a few seconds by a drum that feels like running, and almost every drum feels like running when a hook stings it. Spinning reels used with crankbaits, surface plugs, and jigs that will be cast and retrieved constantly should have the new style of bail that allows it to be opened with the flick of a finger. Daiwa and Shimano both offer a variety of these reels that are reliable and smooth. For surf casters using live or cut bait there is no real need for one of these reels, although the mechanism doesn't hurt anything. You probably can't go with too small a reel when fishing for the big surf reds of autumn. And the smoother the drag the better.

## Line

Big drum demand heavy line, and 50-pound test is common. The new braided lines are starting to get drum anglers' attention since they are thinner than polyfilaments and monofilaments and therefore cast better, and they are just as strong. A shock leader helps sometimes, especially if you are using 30-pound test for drum running in the 50-pound plus category. This system allows a little lighter line, which means more sensitivity and better casting qualities. River and creek drum usually can be handled with 10-pound test.

## Hooks

Spring and autumn drum in the surf are taken on hooks as large as 9/0, down to about a 5/0. Smaller reds require only 1/0 and 2/0. Sharpen those hooks well with a file or hone so that they will sink in quickly.

# Black Drum

Our sounds, bays, large lagoons and even the surf occasionally yield black drum, sometimes of huge size. The average caught in the Carolinas runs about 20 pounds, but they can go as high as 100 pounds or more. Smaller black drum are sometimes mistaken for sheepshead. Cut bait and live shrimp are your best bet, but they will also feed on crabs and clams.

Black drum do not hit as if they are big, but when you set the hook you realize quickly that you have your hands full.

I urge you to release as many drum as possible to protect the resource. However, there is nothing wrong with keeping a few from time to time for the table. Pay attention to the minimum and maximum size limits and the daily bag limit.

# Chapter 4
# Flounder

The flounder is an enigma. With its flat body and beady little eyes on top of its head, it doesn't look as if it would be a fun and popular game fish. But thousands of anglers in the Carolinas will go far out of their way to get a flounder, especially a "door mat" trophy fish that could push eight pounds.

This odd game fish has many attributes. It puts up a good fight; it will hit lures, live bait or cut bait; it tastes delicious; and it can be caught in a wide variety of ways.

The Carolinas offer two primary flounders to anglers: the summer and southern. Once in a while a winter flounder might show up, but these are much more common from Delaware northward to Maine and beyond. The southern and summer flatfish both inhabit somewhat similar bottom types, but the southern is found more frequently along mud bottoms, while the summer prefers sand or a sand-mud mix. Also, the southern flounder will move into fresh-water regions and suffer no ill effects.

From time to time an angler in Carolina waters will haul in a windowpane or gulf flounder. The latter looks almost identical to the summer flounder, but can be distinguished from the summer by looking at the first gill arch. If the lower limb has less than a dozen gillrakers, it's a gulf flounder. If it has more than that (up to 18), it's a summer flounder. Windowpanes are tiny, thin flounder that make good bait but are seldom eaten by people because there just isn't a lot to them.

# Life History

Southern flounder spawn during the winter, with summer flounder usually starting a little earlier but sometimes spawning as late as spring, depending on conditions. The young move into the relative safety of the shallows, but many still fall victim to predators, including other fish and birds. Lagoons with marine vegetation and substantial areas of shallows with sand and mud bottoms are home to the youngsters, and also home in many instances to the adults.

Young flounder do not look at all like the juveniles or adults of the species, for they look much like any other fish when hatched. Each eye is on its own side of the head. But after a few weeks one eye will emigrate to the other side of the head and stay there. During this time the flounder takes on the appearance we all associate with it: a compressed body camouflaged on top and light on bottom.

Flounder do not travel in traditional schools, but will move in loose congregations at the same time into feeding grounds. Individuals decide at about the same time that it is time to move into the surf zone—or wherever they are going to feed. They'll stay in that area until the food becomes scarce, at which time they'll move elsewhere.

Food for southern and summer flounders consists of numerous species of forage fish, with silversides, mullet, shrimp, anchovies, sardines, lizardfish, and the young of other game fish making up their primary diet. They will take bloodworms and sandworms if they present themselves.

# Flounder Tactics

Flounder tactics are simple and straight forward since flounder eat so many things and hit lures, live, and cut bait.

## Soft-Bodied Jigs

Flounder hunt first by smell and then by sight. If they first smell bait in the water, they will more often strike it when it comes by. Soft-bodied jigs of nearly any design or color will fool flounder if they first smell it and it smells real. The odor gets them thinking ambush and convinces them that what they are seeing hopping toward them on the bottom is a real meal. Proof of this is shown when the flounder hits a jig that has been sitting on the bottom in front of it for several seconds, and then hops: they usually strike just as the jig is lifted from the bottom. The flounder has been looking closely at it, smelling

**Shallow water holds nice flounder from spring through fall.**

it all the while. The smell and the fact that it hops around tells the flounder that it can and should be eaten. The shape and color are much less important than the smell and action: if it moves and smells good, it must be food.

So which soft-bodied jigs should you have along on a flounder expedition? Kalin's Silver Lazers; Mister Twister curltails and Sassy Shads; Mann's Stingray, Augertwin, Swimmin' Augertail grubs, and Mosquito Hawks; marabou jigs; feather grubs with soft bodies and whatever else seems appropriate.

## Hard-bodied Jigs

Bucktails and their predecessors have been taking flounder for hundreds of years. The shape of the leadhead doesn't seem to sway the flounder one way or another. Soak the bucktail in fish attractant and you will take more than those anglers who don't.

47

**Various small jigs are always something to have at hand for flounder.**

## Crankbaits

The original Rapala minnow (floating model) retrieved slowly and steadily just off the bottom, with the occasional one-second pause so that the lure begins to rise, is one of the most effective methods for using crankbaits for flounder. No, I suppose it doesn't have to be a Rapala: any such floating crankbait would probably do the trick, but I usually use the Rapala because of its lifelike action. If the lure imitates a mud minnow, silverside, mullet or other bait fish, try it.

## Surface Plugs

In water that is clear and slick, and less than 18 inches deep, you can have some fun with flounder by using surface plugs. Any deeper, or if the flounder's visibility is restricted due to choppy water or water that has a lot of sediment in suspension, and you won't have much luck. The same plugs used for reds will suffice for flounder.

## Live, Dead, and Cut Bait

A small, live finger mullet or similar forage fish drifted over flounder territory or retrieved through it from shore is a tough bait to beat, especially

**Success in the surf for a tasty flounder.**

when you can see bait fish in the water. The presence of bait fish in the water triggers the flounder's feeding response and gets it in the mood, so when it sees your bait coming along it acts instinctively and strikes when it comes within range. Try a walleye method: attach a live or dead bait fish to a walleye jig head and retrieve it across the bottom.

Cut bait drifted over sand or hard mud bottoms, or a whole dead mud minnow or finger mullet will work. So will squid and bloodworms or sandworms.

# Hot Spots
## In The Surf

One day a few summers ago I decided to prove once and for all (to myself) that flounder prefer certain spots in the surf where food is funneled to them. I suspected that they liked the troughs created in the sand by the waves, because it made sense to me that the wave action would knock the finger mullet I was watching into them. *If I were a flounder*, I thought, *I'd lie in the sand in the trough and wait for unlucky mullet to be pushed over the lip of the trough right onto me, then I'd nail them.*

The wave action was not allowing me to really tell exactly where my bait was, since the troughs were so shallow, so I put on a face mask and snorkeled out into the surf. The water was shallow—only a few feet deep—and the visibility wasn't too bad, so I was able to see the bottom for a few yards in each direction.

49

**The flounder is a regular from piers, too.**

**Work the troughs in the surf zone.**

Sure enough, every 10 or 12 yards I spotted a flounder lying on the bottom, always on the inside of the trough. They would scoot as soon as I appeared, but I had proved to myself that they do want to be in one certain spot in relation to the wave action. It was annoying to come to my bait lying on the bottom—a live finger mullet—and see a large flounder tugging furiously on it. By the time I got back onto the beach and grabbed the rod, the flounder was long gone.

Small sections of sand between points and spits often hold numerous flounder. Any area of the beach that has structure with sand or hard mud in between should be explored. Go at low tide and look for these spots, mark them somehow, and then return later to fish them.

**Waiting for a door mat.**

Don't make the mistake of casting into a yard of water, then quickly reeling in. Flounder are frequently caught in very shallow water. Remember, they are flat as a board and can get into only inches of water if they want to. I had this point driven home one morning while fishing with George Misko in a coastal river.

We were having touch-and-go results working the little rivulets that fed the river from the lagoon bordering the river, so we decided to hit the cuts on each end of the bridge. I cast up against one of the stanchions into about 10 inches of water—no more. I hopped my white paddletail grub once, and let it settle on the bottom beside a rock outcropping.

Just as I picked it up, a 15-inch flounder whacked it and ran toward the rocks and stanchion. I turned him just before he made it, and a minute later had him in the net after a quick and accurate scoop by George. We were both surprised to see so big a flounder in so shallow a spot, and continued to work the shallows hard. This tactic paid big dividends.

**Britta Newman prefers an ultralight rig for creek flounder.**

## In Rivers And Creeks

It is harder to determine bottom composition in rivers and creeks than on the beach. A chart showing the bottom is invaluable, and I recommend you buy one for each river you fish.

Although bottom conditions do change somewhat from season to season, these changes are not so pronounced as those experienced by beaches and surf zones. If the bottom in one spot is hard mud one year, it will probably be hard mud the next. However, dredging in the mouths of rivers can radically change bottom composition, so ask around to see if the dredger has been working certain areas. The local bait and tackle shop owners will know, as will the Coast Guard.

The edges of currents are where you should try first.

Flounder want the food to come to them: they are not prowlers like seatrout, bluefish, and reds. Flounders hunt by ambush and surprise and don't want their meal going by them too quickly. Yes, flounder are sometimes taken by still fishing, but you will greatly increase your success rate if you keep the bait moving.

The mouths of small feeder creeks and rivers where the bottom is mud or sand are excellent spots to look for flounder. As with surf casting for them, use a live finger mullet or silverside dragged or hopped slowly across the bottom. You can rig a live bait fish in many ways. You may want to use a tandem rig with a bucktail or soft-bodied jig above a live finger mullet or lizardfish below.

## Lagoons, Backwaters, And The Intracoastal Waterway

Lagoons with feeder creeks and little estuaries joining them can hold lots of flounder, especially if the water is calm and clear. Broad flats don't hold as many flounder as do the edges with moving water.

**Boats and waders mix in the Intracoastal for autumn flounder.**

53

## From Piers

Pier anglers take countless flounder along the Carolinas' coasts. Summer is the best time for flounder no matter where and how you are fishing for them, and the summer pier anglers position themselves over the surf zone and lower finger mullet to the flounder below.

**Rods line the pier hoping for action on a warm autumn afternoon.**

**Inlets are prime flounder habitat.**

# Flounder Tackle

For the most part you can use the same tackle employed for seatrout, that is, light to medium light gear.

## Rods

For the surf, select a rod that has a little more backbone so that you can cast additional weight into the wind. A stouter rod is also needed for the pier so that you can haul "door mats" up over the rail without undue strain on the rod. River and creek rods need be no different from trout rods used for the same places.

## Reels

Your trout reels will work for flounder, too.

## Lines

Some flounder have serious teeth, and you may want to use a modest shock leader or slightly heavier line. Other than that, your trout line will do.

## Hooks

When using live, dead or cut bait, 1/0 and 2/0 hooks are best.

**A bottom rig for flounder can be made or bought in a tackle shop.**

## Terminal Rigs

Just as in most other instances, the simpler the terminal rig the better.

With flounder beginning to turn on in the late spring and staying around until autumn, the season is long and fun. Only the hottest summer weather tends to put them off the bite. Their populations are stable, but don't overdo it and take more than your fair share.

**A respectable flounder taken on medium light tackle.**

# Chapter 5
# Tarpon

The awesome tarpon may have been the Carolinas' best kept secret, but now the word is getting out that *Megalops atlanticus* is alive and well in the warm waters of the Carolina summer. As the heat of the summer drives the inshore water temperature up into the low 80s, the tarpon show up in the sounds and rivers to feed on mullet and other forage fish in the shallow waters. Only a relative few anglers know that the tarpon comes here starting around the middle of July and stays until the middle of August (sometimes a little later if the water stays pleasantly warm), but organizations are starting to get serious about tarpon tournaments or "rodeos," and that is spreading the word. North Carolina had its first tarpon tourney in August of 1993, hosted by the Oriental Rotary Club.

## Life History

Like the ladyfish and bonefish, the tarpon has strange looking young that resemble eels. Born at sea (a female tarpon may pay out 12 million or so eggs), they drift with the current toward shore, where they take up residence in the shallows and undergo a metamorphosis that turns them into tiny tarpon. They grow slowly when compared to bluefish.

As they grow on the flats and in the channels and mangrove swamps of Florida and Central and South America, "baby" tarpon provide great sport on light tackle. When they get bigger, they begin to migrate northward, and tarpon well over 100 pounds have been fought from piers and boats in both Carolinas.

Unfortunately, most anglers who hook a tarpon here are not prepared for what happens next, namely an *Oh-My-Gawd!* run that sees the "silver king" exploding from the water with repeated, back-to-back twisting and spinning leaps. Most are broken off before the angler has time to react. Usually the angler was fishing for king mackerel and hooked the tarpon accidentally while trolling live bait or fishing from the end of a pier.

Tarpon like fresh water as well as salt, and are frequently found in great numbers in brackish water. Bass anglers casting crankbaits in the fresh-water reaches of rivers that have salt below have had sudden, brief, and exciting encounters with big tarpon that gulped their silver or chrome Rat-L-Trap and rocketed out of the water only to sever the flimsy line. These anglers sometimes see a tarpon roll on the surface and mistake it for a large bass, which they then cast to and hook. When a tarpon rolls on the surface, it is not feeding but taking air into its air bladder.

# Tarpon Tactics

Television fishing shows usually portray tarpon anglers fishing during the day, and they do take quite a few tarpon as they change location from channel to estuary, flat to channel, mangrove creek to cut. Guides know when and where "their" tarpon are moving, and position their clients or "sports" between the two spots and either sight fish for them, or dangle favorite baits in the depths where the tarpon are known to wait. (The latter method is typified by guides who anchor in Florida's prolific Boca Grande Pass on the Gulf coast and lower crabs to the huge tarpon below.) But the fact is that tarpon do most of their feeding at night, and anglers who have mastered night fishing take many more tarpon than those who haven't.

Carolinas' sounds, larger estuaries, and broad rivers are tarpon country. Trolling large crankbaits and lipped minnows, or sight casting to tarpon rolling on the surface (provided you know where they tend to do such things; some locales are better than others to view this activity) are the best ways to produce strikes.

## Lures and Plugs

It would be ludicrous to give you a list of tarpon lures by name and color. Tarpon eat so many different things that nearly any lure could conceivably catch a tarpon under the right conditions. Most anglers new to tarpon fishing and without the benefit of a guide or fellow angler who has tarpon experience

**A large tarpon taken in close with a Rat-L-Trap crankbait.**

make the mistake of retrieving lures too quickly: they know that tarpon are powerful swimmers and jumpers and wrongly assume that they want a fast-moving bait all the time. This is not the case.

The best way I can describe the speed of a tarpon retrieve is "average"—not too fast, and not so slow that the tarpon gets a real good look at what you are trying to fool him with. Yellow, white, silver, and red lures that present an easy target for the tarpon, which doesn't assault a lure but rather eases up behind it and "mouths" the bait in a surprisingly gentle manner, are often the best choice. A tarpon will come up from under a bait fish or lure that is imitating one, arching over it with its mouth agape and inhaling it. It usually continues this motion so that it ends up going back down with the lure in its mouth. This motion often makes strikes difficult to detect, and many tarpon are lost before they are ever felt, which explains the popularity and effectiveness of sight fishing: if you can see the tarpon take your bait it is easier to hook it.

Tarpon have tough mouths that require a vigorous setting of the hook. You must really drive the hook home if you want to get the fish to the boat. Otherwise, the hook will come free during a run or jump.

## Live Bait

A finger mullet or similarly sized forage fish will take a baby tarpon just as quickly as it will take a triple-digit tarpon. Herring, menhaden, silversides, blue crabs (and other crabs, too), croakers, small drum, lizardfish, and a wide variety of other marine fishes are eaten by tarpon. In the Carolinas you will most often see finger mullet being trolled slowly or drifted to attract this fish, but if you can get some nice crabs and work a cut between two islands or shoals, do so.

# Hot Spots

Only a tiny percentage of anglers plying the inshore waters of the Carolinas are after tarpon or know how and where to go after them. This is going to change with time as more tournaments are held. Now, though, if you were to come alongside another angler and ask if he has seen or caught any tarpon today, he'll likely look at you like you are some kind of nut.

But there are other ways of finding tarpon. Devote your time to covering territory until you find them. Starting with trolling in the inlets and sounds, and in the lower reaches of large rivers such as the Neuse, White Oak, Cape Fear, Pamlico, and New in North Carolina, and Combahee, Cooper, and Santee in South Carolina. Sounds that should be covered are South Carolina's Port Royal and St. Helena, and North Carolina's Pamlico, Albemarle, Bogue, and Core. Try South Carolina's Bulls Bay, Stono Inlet, Winyah Bay, and in the cut between Bull and Capers Islands. North Carolina's Shallotte, Brown's, Ocracoke, Oregon, New River, Rich, Corncake, and Bogue Inlets are all worth a try.

Finally, be careful when the tarpon is close to the boat. A 75-pound tarpon can kill you if you are not cautious and respectful of its size and strength. There are verified reports of tarpon killing anglers who failed to take caution when boating a big fish. Not only can such a fish jump suddenly and knock you into the transom or overboard, its leaps often attract sharks. Always watch where you put your hands when releasing tarpon.

# Tarpon Tackle

When dealing with a fish that enjoys the reputation of being one of the top five fighting fish in the world and that can easily go more than 100 pounds, you must—must!—choose your tackle carefully and with much forethought. As in any other type of fishing, it is not so much the species you are after that dictates the design of the tackle needed as it is the situation in which you are fishing.

## Rods

The novice might believe that a tremendous game fish such as the tarpon would require a rod similar in length to those used in the surf for drum of equal

Courtesy of DuPont Stren

**Rods have to be able to handle extreme stress from these fighting game fish.**

weight. Not so. Most tarpon rods are fairly short, with boat rods staying around 6 feet in length and spinning rods going around 7 feet. Seldom do you see longer rods at work in these respective cases. There just isn't any need for them. A shorter, fast or ultrafast action rod can deal with a tarpon provided it has a thick enough base and perhaps a fore-grip which allows the angler to get more leverage on the fish.

A selection of good tarpon rods for trolling include: Lamiglas's Model E660, a 6-foot, fast action rod that handles 15-to 40-pound test; Fenwick's Seahawk Pacific Model SP 660 C, a 6-foot rod meant for 20- to 50-pound test line, and their Atlanticstik Supreme Model ASBT 60 H that handles 20- to 40-pound test and is also a 6-footer; and Shakespeare's Contender Ranger Model 1960 CH, a 6-footer that takes 30- to 50-pound test line.

Spinning rods for tarpon would include: Lamiglas's Model E865S, a 6-foot 6-inch fast action rod for 15- to 40-pound test (this one is on the light side and is for anglers who have some experience handling big tarpon on lighter rods); and any rod recommended by Biscayne Rod Manufacturing of Hialeah, Florida, one of the nation's premier tarpon rod makers.

## Reels

Any tarpon reel should offer a drag made to the highest standards and a retrieve ratio that allows you to take up line quickly. Extreme pressures are put on reels that do business with tarpon, and a reel that might be considered marginal for lesser game fish is probably unsuited for tarpon.

Trolling and boat reels that will serve you well are: Penn's Models 113H and 114H. These two classic reels are for 30- and 50-pound test line respectively, and hold plenty of it. They even have harness clamps for that special tarpon that comes along and wants to tow your boat to Africa; Penn's International Models 20T (new on the market), 30TW, and 50T (these hold 750 yards of 20-pound test, 900 yards of 30-pound test, and 850 yards of 50-pound test, respectively; and Penn's 330GTI, an "economy" reel that is a bargain and holds 350 yards of 30-pound test line; a light reel for seasoned tarpon anglers is Shimano's TR2000LD that holds 300 yards of 20-pound test.

For spinning rods, a few good reels are: Penn's Model 850SS (350 yards of 20-pound test); Shimano's Baitrunner Model 6500A (185 yards of 30-pound test; you better know what you are doing with this one, since it holds less than 200 yards of 30-pound test line); and Shakespeare's Alpha Model 570 (holds 270 yards of 20-pound test line).

**A Penn levelwind reel loaded for pier tarpon.**

## Lines

Polyfilaments and braids are the way to go once again with a fish like the tarpon. Many guides recommend Stren Kevlar, Fenwick Iron Thread, and Berkley Ultramax. And many outdoors writers are getting on the braided line bandwagon, too, such as Ken Schultz, one of *Field & Stream* magazine's contributing editors and a highly respected angler.

The sensitivity of braided lines is especially important when dealing with tarpon since they tend to strike very lightly. Even when sight fishing, line sensitivity often means the difference between success and missed opportunity. My two favorite braids are Stren Kevlar and Fenwick Iron Thread. I must warn you, though, that you should avoid setting the hook on a tarpon too hard when using braided line, despite the fish's notoriously hard mouth. Though I seriously doubt you could ever break one of the aforementioned rods because of too strong a set, a less reliable rod could possibly snap or crack. A firm set, yes. A rip-your-head-off set, no.

Never, never use generic line for tarpon. Go with Trilene, Stren, or Ande, the latter of which currently boasts more than a dozen International Game Fish Association line & tippet class records for tarpon, including one 283-pounder.

If you are using light line for tarpon, say around 15- or 20-pound test, seriously consider a shock leader. Tarpon have armored bodies that can fray the line during the fight, and a shock leader can do a lot to prevent it from breaking.

## Hooks

Hook selection is more important when fishing for tarpon than it is for other species such as seatrout, pompano, and flounder. An armored mouth requires a hook equal to the task, so you must select wisely or end up frustrated.

Any hook that can bend, will. The hook you use for a bass worm will not suffice for a big tarpon. Stainless steel is needed, and you must take the time to make 100% sure that the hook just can't get any sharper. Replace any questionable hooks that came on the lures you bought with stainless steel if you have to. Sharpen every treble hook.

# Chapter 6
# King and Spanish Mackerel

No fish in the inshore waters of the Carolinas' coasts draws crowds like the king mackerel. Dozens of king mackerel tournaments in the two states offer almost unbelievable purses. Anglers from all over the South come to get in on the action.

But it's not just tournaments that bring them. With a game fish that comes in big numbers, fights like mad, and weighs up to 90 pounds (the IGFA all-tackle world record was caught by Norton I. Thomton in Key West on February 16, 1976, and weighed 90 pounds), it is small wonder that anglers go a little nuts when the kings show up in the spring after wintering in Florida waters.

Then there is the spanish mackerel, which isn't as big as a king but is sought after with nearly as much enthusiasm. Lovely to look at, the spanish is a fighter that will put you to the test on medium light tackle. It inhabits the same waters as the king, and, like the king, can be caught from pier, jetty, and boat.

Both are excellent eating, and are not nearly so oily as the little Atlantic mackerel that is so popular in the summer along the coast of New England.

## Life History

Mackerel are constantly on the move, and the young can be found roving from place to place just as do the adults. Water temperature is important with these transient fish, and once it gets cold for good they'll be gone for the season. Usually showing up around April and May, they stay well into the fall and even into winter if temperatures remains mild. The fastest fishing occurs in May and June and in September and early October.

King and spanish mackerel are predators that hunt schools of menhaden, mullet, pinfish, and other forage fish that swim in schools and present good targets. Fast swimmers, they hunt from the surface down to 100 feet. Spanish, however, are more likely to be caught near the surface.

A king mackerel over 40 pounds is called a "smoker" because of the way it can strip a reel of line so fast that it "smokes." Kings hit bait fish and lures from below and can come completely out of the water on the strike. It is especially exciting to see a big one rocket out of the water as it hits a bait trolled or drifted near the surface.

Females will go to about 40 pounds, but seldom much more. Males sometimes run up to 80 pounds, and you really see some beauties when the boats come in from tournaments.

Inshore waters in the Carolinas see the best king and spanish fishing in the spring as the mackerel work in close to the beaches. Pier anglers take them regularly then, usually from the end of the pier. Summer is up and down, with stalls in the action usually coming with extra-hot weather.

# Mackerel Tactics

How and where to fish for mackerel is no great secret, but it is obvious that some anglers are much more accomplished than others, especially when it comes to the Big Daddy kings. Since mackerel are predators that hunt forage fish—and will eat a wide variety of them—you would think that all you need do is troll a fresh, live bait fish and you'll soon have plenty of action. Sure, there are days when it really is that easy, but mackerel are sometimes tough to find. You must have a plan and know exactly what you are doing to catch many kings and spanish.

# For Kings
## Lures

Reefs, drop-offs, ledges and wrecks are where you want to start your search by trolling any lure that imitates a forage fish. Use your Loran and depth finder to locate and examine the structure or radical bottom variation and then troll in an erratic pattern back and forth over the area. Using several rods set at different depths using downriggers and planers is one way of finding what level the kings are at, but do not expect a school of large kings

**Trolling rods need not be overly long for kings.**

since most big ones are loners. The smaller ones running between 5 and 25 pounds will travel in schools.

## Crankbaits

Large Rebel, Rapala, Rat-L-Trap, Spots, Flatfish, Wally Divers, Bomber Long "A"s, and similar crankbaits all catch kings. Strike King's Diamond Shad should prove worthwhile. Colors should mimic those of the prevalent bait fish, so pay attention to what is in the water at the time.

## Spoons

There are so many good trolling spoons today that it is hard to know which to mention, but a few to try are Mann's Loudmouth Rattling spoon in various chrome combinations; Krocodile spoons in the same shades and maybe the chrome blue prism lite; Daredevles in silver, gold, and blue tints; Rapala's new Minnow Spoon in blue shad, gold, and chrome; and Luhr Jensen's crippled Herring spoons. When trolling at fast speeds near the surface, check the spoon's action frequently to make sure it is behaving correctly. Some go haywire at fast speeds.

## Natural Baits

One of the most effective live baits for king mackerel is a menhaden. The size of these bait fish varies depending on the size of king you want: if you are after smokers you'll want a 10 to 15-inch bait; a smaller one if you are after schoolies. Besides menhaden, ballyhoo, pinfish, "snapper" bluefish, spots, and other forage fish are used with great success. Ballyhoo are normally store-bought, but you can collect your own menhaden, pinfish, snapper blues and spots. The latter three bait fish can be caught with ease from any pier with a small hook and a strip of squid or flounder belly jiggled near the pilings. Use a light weight rod and have a cooler with aerator handy to drop them in. Menhaden are best caught while they are schooling in the manner described in Chapter Two. Chumming with bait fish chunks and pieces is common.

Finger mullet can be used for kings, too, and you can get them easily with a cast net.

King mackerel baits are often dressed with a King Buster or similar skirt that is brightly colored and gets the king's attention. These are inexpensive and come in many color schemes.

# For Spanish

## Lures

Spanish are known for being unreasonable when it comes to lures. Sometimes they want only a specific one and will swim right past anything else. Spanish mackerel buffs have tackle boxes crammed with all kinds of lures because of this. But you will find that experienced spanish anglers all have a handful of lures in common. These are the ones that produce when the going is slow year after year, and can take a spanish even when the weather gets hopelessly hot enough to keep mackerel from biting.

## Crankbaits

The Rattlin' Rogue in chrome/black back looks and acts just like a finger mullet and is devastating on spanish mackerel. Bomber's B7 Mullet in silver/blue/white is also a big hit with spanish. In addition to these crankbaits, try: Storm's Thunderstick; Rebel and Rapala minnows; Rat-L-Traps; and Hell-benders. Do not hesitate to try any crankbait that looks as if it might work. Spanish are funny about being picky one day and ravenous the next to the point that they don't seem to care about what is in the water just as long as it looks edible. Any spoon is good, too.

**Spanish mackerel anglers work a Carolina pier.**

## The Got-Cha Plug

More spanish mackerel are caught on Got-Cha plugs than any other lure. It seems as though every tackle shop in the coastal Carolinas carries a large selection of these strange looking plugs. They come in many body and hook colors (spanish are fond of Got-Cha plugs with gold hooks), and different sizes, too. Some have tails, others don't. They are inexpensive, so you can buy several and not break the bank. If I could only have one spanish mackerel lure for casting, trolling, and jigging, it would be a 3-inch, 1700 series Sea Striker Got-Cha plug with a gold body, gold hooks, and a yellow head.

**Rods of all sizes can be seen on Carolina piers when the mackerel are in.**

## Soft-bodied Jigs

Yellow, white, chartreuse and silver soft-bodied jigs with curltails are another good lure for spanish. Cast them out and retrieve them with a jerking motion, or troll them and work the rod. The action of the tail on a curltail jig looks very much like a tail of a small bait fish.

## Hard-bodied Jigs

Bucktails, bonito "feathers," and marabou jigs aren't used as often as soft-bodied jigs nowadays, but in days gone by, before the soft-bodies became popular, these jigs took lots of spanish mackerel. I prefer a marabou or bonito feather to a standard bucktail.

## Natural Baits

Silversides, pinfish, finger mullet, and the young of many other fish that inhabit spanish mackerel territory are all fair game to this fighter. Mud minnows will serve in a pinch, too. Your baits should be smaller than the average king mackerel bait, 3 to 6 inches or so.

**Pinfish are excellent bait for large spanish mackerel.**

**Spanish will follow a trawler, making finding them easier for anglers.**

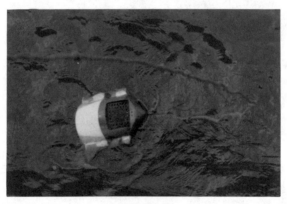

**A rope and live bait bucket are standard gear for pier anglers using live bait for macks.**

# Hot Spots

Since mackerel are always moving around, a hot spot on Monday may be stone cold on Tuesday. Having a number of potential hot spots is best.

# For Kings

King mackerel have a clear preference for greenish water. They are open-water fish, remember, so they feel more comfortable—and therefore more likely to feed—if they are in water that is natural to them. Inshore fishing for kings is therefore best when the high tide brings in water from seaward that has a green tint to it. Also, this is of a higher salinity, and kings like that.

## From Piers

May and June in the Carolinas will find king mackerel specialists working the ends of long piers with specialized tackle. They'll show up long before dawn on the incoming tide and stake out positions for themselves. When a king is hooked at the end of the pier (not all piers allow king mackerel fishing because of the problems the unruly fish can cause for others) anglers try their best to get out of way of the person who is fighting the big fish. Well, most do. Others do not take kindly to being asked to hastily move themselves and their rods to make way for another angler trying to get the best of a fish that seems bent on wrapping itself in every line on the pier.

## In Mouths of Rivers And Channels

On high tides the kings will come into the mouths of rivers and channels to intercept bait fish milling there. Trolling through the green water where the river's current slackens is smart.

## Offshore

You can be offshore a ways (within sight of land) and still be considered within inshore waters. Kings patrol the waters a couple of miles offshore, and boaters harvest thousands every season by trolling and drifting baits in these areas. Watch the depth finder for dips and troughs, an inshore wreck, debris, or a natural or artificial reef. Watch the other boats, too.

# For Spanish

The same advice for kings applies to spanish since they, too, move around constantly.

## From Piers

The farther out you get on the pier, the better. Spanish do not like heavy surf and shallow water. They prefer to hunt in swells or less raucous waters where they can see what is going on around them.

## In The Mouths of Rivers And Channels

Spanish mackerel will come in a little closer than kings, and they also like to stay near channel buoys where small bait fish hide. Early to mid-morning and late-afternoon to evening hours are best for spanish no matter where you are. Use a long rod that can cast a good ways so you can reach passing schools feeding on the surface (watch for bait fish scattering on the surface and birds feeding on the school).

## Offshore

You can find spanish more than a dozen miles from the beach, but usually there is no need to go that far out. Most of the time you'll be able to find a school within a few miles of shore.

Use binoculars to watch where the other boats are heading, and keep an eye out for flocks of birds working the water surface. Avoid trolling too close to a school or through it, because spanish are afraid of boats and will dive to escape. Approach the school quartering from the front and stop short but close enough to reach them with a good cast. Cast in front of the school so that the lure can be brought right into it at a quick pace. Or approach slowly from the front and turn the boat behind and perpendicularly toward the school as you pass the rear. This maneuver will bring a trolled lure through the school. Increase your speed so that the lure is moving fast as soon as you make the turn behind the school. Spoons work well in all these situations, with Hopkins, Kastmasters, Krocodiles, Clark spoons, Weeping Willows, and Mooselook Wobblers bringing good results (order the latter two spoons from L.L. Bean).

If you see a trawler going by, troll behind it if the nets aren't being used. Spanish will swarm behind these boats picking off the bait fish there.

# Mackerel Tackle

Your king and spanish gear are going to be different.

# For Kings

## Rods

For boat action, medium to medium heavy boat rods in the 6-to 7-foot category are preferred. For the pier you will need longer rods that can get the bait out there, however nothing longer than 8 feet. Daiwa, Penn, and Shimano all make several rods that are well-suited for king mackerel, and they aren't overly expensive.

## Reels

Kings are runners, so you either use a spinning reel with a deep spool and an outstanding drag, or a levelwind with the same attributes. The reel in king mackerel fishing is probably more important than the rod, so if you are going to cut corners anywhere, do it on the rod. Penn's Model 309M, 45 GLS, and 25GLS are all sound choices. Whichever reel you choose for kings, make sure it holds plenty of line (at least 300 yards, preferably 400).

### Line and Hooks

Kings and spanish have teeth that are like needles, and they can sever a line instantly. You should always use a shock or steel wire leader to prevent this. Even small mackerel can bite through a relatively heavy line with no problem. And kings have a way of slashing at line with their tails.

Kings deserve 20- to 50-pound test polyfilament or braid. A multistrand wire leader 5 to 6 feet long is needed, or a heavy shock leader.

Kings rate 2/0 to 8/0 stainless steel hooks, depending on the size of fish in the area.

# For Spanish

## Rods and Reels

Just use the same ones you use for drum, etc. Don't buy a special rod or reel for these fish.

### Line and Hooks

Spanish should get 10- to 15-pound test and a shorter leader that is 24 inches long and about 20-pound test. Spanish hooks can go smaller, around a 1/0 or 2/0.

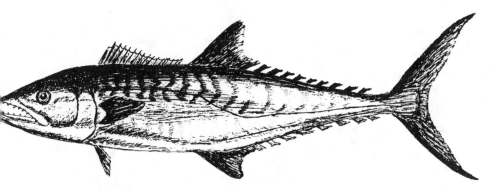

**King mackerel.**

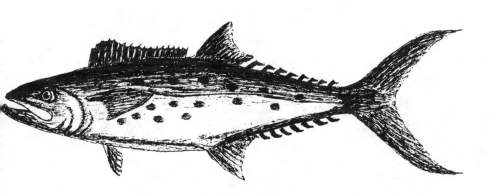

**Spanish mackerel.**

# Chapter 7
# Cobia

The only reason the cobia is not more popular in the Carolinas is because of the king mackerel.

For some reason the king is just that—the king—around here, but to tell you the truth, the cobia is just as hard a hitter—some would say harder—and the fight these beautiful game fish put up is nothing other than extraordinary.

When a cobia hits a lure or bait, it will turn on every bit of energy it can muster, burn up your reel, jump from time to time, and otherwise go wild. Even small cobia are a challenge, and on light tackle they can wreak havoc on the angler and his gear.

Although the cobia spends most of its time near the bottom, oddly, most caught in the Carolinas are taken near the surface.

Why?

Because cobia are easier to find near the surface inshore: find a buoy, pallet, mat of seaweed, or other piece of flotsam floating on the surface and you stand a good chance of finding a cobia.

These are structure-oriented fish that hunt by ambush. Cobia hide in the shadows of anything available—even boats—then slam into prey that wanders by. And they eat whatever happens along—crabs, all sorts of fish, shrimp, eels—whatever presents itself.

Because cobia often move in loose schools, if you catch one, you might be able to get another from the same spot.

I don't know a fish that tastes better than a cobia, and I recommend you keep one once in a while for dinner.

# Life History

Spawning in late summer and fall after feeding heavily from spring throughout the summer, cobia show up in inshore waters along the Carolinas starting in June. By July they are here in force and will lurk in the outer mouths of larger rivers, channels, and near piers until fall when cooling water sends them south.

Cobia here run on the average between 15 and 50 pounds, with larger fish in the 100-pound range being caught from time to time. The IGFA all-tackle world record was set by Peter Goulding on July 9, 1985, with a 135-pound 9-ounce cobia off Shark Bay in Western Australia. This tremendous fish doesn't surprise me, because I have seen similar specimens hanging at the mouth of Fremantle Harbor below Perth in Western Australia near the sea and channel buoys.

If you think the cobia looks unusual, you are right. It is the sole member of its family (Rachycentridae). This makes it easy to identify, with its beautiful coloration of dark and light brown, and its peculiar fins and body shape.

# Cobia Tactics

Cobia are ambushers with a broad sense of taste: they like lots of everything. But don't assume you will always have an easy time catching them. Cobia do not take well to hunger and like to keep a full stomach. This means that you are going to have to offer them something that they just can't refuse.

## Lures

When hungry, cobia readily fall for lures cast or trolled past their outposts at all depths. There is no need to go out and buy special cobia lures, because what you use for king mackerel, bluefish, and large drum will work just fine for cobia.

## Live And Cut Bait

One of the surest ways to entice a cobia—even a full one—is to use the liveliest bait you can find. A jumpy pinfish, spot, menhaden, jumbo shrimp, croaker, or even a small seatrout will get its attention. The key is to make the bait easily available by drifting it near the spot where the cobia is lurking. The Newman Rig described in Chapter 2 is a good one for this, or you can nose hook the bait. Shrimp can be hooked in the traditional manner, but make sure you use the biggest, scaredest one you can find. Toss it up-current and let it drift right past. A cobia is almost certain to grab it.

# Hot Spots

George Misko

**Finger mullet and crabs can take cobia in the surf, too.**

In addition to hanging over wrecks and reefs, under boats, beneath piers, debris, and buoys, cobia sometimes come right to the beach in the dead of summer and startle surf casters trying for blues. Imagine thinking you are going to catch a 5-pound bluefish when suddenly a 50-pound cobia eats your bait and tries to drag you off the beach!

## From A Boat

Start by asking around where the cobia have been hitting. If reports are sketchy, start at the first channel buoy in a river's mouth. As you approach the buoy, get the sun behind you and look under and around the buoy for the shadow or silhouette of a cobia. Check the current and use it to bring the live bait past the fish, or troll a good lure around the buoy. Another way is to get the boat up current, cut the motor, and drift past the buoy casting plugs and crankbaits.

If that buoy doesn't pay off, move to the next. Don't skip smaller buoys thinking no fish will be beneath them, because cobia will hide under small buoys as well as large ones. And you can take a surprisingly large cobia from a small buoy.

After working the buoys, start looking for flotsam such as boards, pallets, or anything else that makes shade. When you go by anchored or drifting boats, check beneath them. If you see a cobia there, troll past it. When you catch a cobia beneath another angler's boat, get it in fast and then leave at high speed, 'cause he probably ain't gonna be happy.

Just as dolphin hide beneath seaweed mats, so do cobia. It's tough to see all the way beneath a large mat, though. Try letting a live menhaden run around near the edge of the mat and under it if possible.

Keep that depth finder on and look for reefs and wrecks, even if they are small. A live pinfish or other bait fish dropped onto the reef will often produce. Also check bridge pilings.

### From Piers

Few specialists work piers for cobia, and most caught from piers are taken by king mackerel anglers and light tackle anglers trying for croaker, snapper blues, and spot. These smaller fish are often attacked by the cobia as the angler reels them in, and the fight and fury at the end of the pier is something to see when a 35-pound cobia grabs a snapper blue on light tackle and makes for the horizon.

## Cobia Tackle

Since most cobia are caught from boats by drifting, trolling, and casting baits, you will want a versatile rod unless you have the cash to buy a different rod for each method. I don't have that kind of money, so I use one rod. It's a Shakespeare BWS 2200, a 7-foot medium light rod armed with 20- or 30-pound test Stren Super Tough or equally strong line. This rod lets me do it all, and I love it. Similar rods might include Penn's Gold Cup in 8-foot, medium action with 25-pound test, or Daiwa's Sealine SG623, which is a 7-foot beauty that can take 12- to 30-pound test.

### Reels

Spinning reels for cobia must have a serious drag and major line capacity, like Daiwa's Black Gold Model BG90 that holds 225 yards of 30-pound test;

Shimano's Baitrunner Model BTR6500A (at the bare minimum of line capacity); and Abu-Garcia's Cardinal Gold Max Model GM9 (an excellent value for the price).

## Line

Line for cobia should be especially stretch resistant because of the cobia's habit of allowing itself to be easily reeled in the first time, only to suddenly take off at boatside. I warn you not to ever—EVER—gaff a cobia the first time it comes up to the boat and bring it on board. Like big bluefish and smoker kings, a 50-pound cobia will break every piece of gear it gets near if it is still strong and angry.

Lines should be anywhere from 15- to 40-pound test or so, depending on the average size of the cobia in the area. Shock leaders and multistrand steel wire leaders are used.

**Inlets with lots of current carrying bait fish out to sea have cobia hanging at the mouths.**

## Hooks

Use the same hooks you do for large blues or kings.

Anytime you're heading out for a day of fishing, or returning, don't motor past that buoy, flotsam, or drifting seaweed, without pausing to try for a cobia. They'll make your reel scream, your arms ache, your heart thump, and your stomach happy.

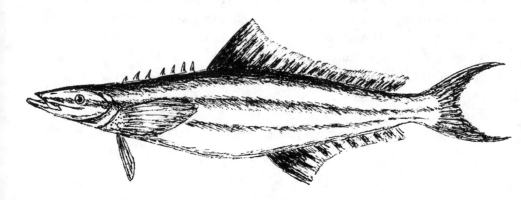

**Cobia.**

# Chapter 8
# Sheepshead

The sheepshead is a tough, powerful fish with a small army of devotees along the Carolinas' coasts.

Fish of structure, they can be found around pilings, piers, bridges, wharves, and oyster beds. They are one of the most maddeningly picky game fish in our waters, and they have a way of breaking off once on the hook by rubbing the line against the structure they were near.

A member of the porgy family, which includes porgies, pinfish, and scups, the sheepshead of the Carolinas is not related to the California sheepshead, which is a wrasse (and the name is spelled differently, too).

Sheepshead caught in Carolina waters average about a pound, but those anglers who have become experts in fishing for them know where and how to find 5-pounders with regularity. Still, catching even a small sheepshead on light tackle is thrilling because it will try every trick in the book to wrap your line over or around pilings and rocks covered with sharp barnacles.

Sheepshead often can be fished by sight. You can bring them up for a look by chumming with tiny pieces of shrimp, crushed crabs, diced fish, minced clams, or the like. Watch what they do when they see something that interests them: they will swim up to it and look it over before eating it. They are curious but cautious.

If you want to set a new IGFA all-tackle world record, you are going to have to beat the 21-pound 4-ounce sheepshead that Wayne Desselle took on April 16, 1982, in Bayou St. John in New Orleans.

# Life History

Sheepshead spawn offshore. The eggs hatch and the tiny fish move toward shore to hide around piers and other structure where their parents forage, though they have no idea which sheepshead are their parents, of course. They have nothing to fear from larger sheepshead because they do not eat fish. However, spanish mackerel, bluefish, and other predators will eat them, so the young fish stick tight to the structure.

Sheepshead grow somewhat slowly, but may reach 3 feet in length. They do not migrate per se, but will change locations if food runs low, or the water gets too cold. They head seaward when time comes to breed.

Although territorial, sheepshead tolerate a certain number and size range of other sheepshead in their territory. A sheepshead you see working some old pier pilings one week will likely be there the next, and the next, unless someone or something eats it. They are creatures of habit.

I once watched a lone sheepshead work a set of old pier pilings in the same pattern for four days. He would start at one end of the demolished pier and work his way to the other end, then swim up the back and start all over again, happily munching on barnacles that he crushed with his prominent teeth, as well as small crabs clinging to the debris, and the occasional tiny shrimp that drifted by. I tried every trick in the book, but couldn't get him to bite. He is still there as far as I know, probably annoying anglers on a regular basis. I estimated his weight at 15 pounds.

# Sheepshead Tactics

Find a jetty, oyster bed, pier, pilings, inshore wreck or other barnacle-encrusted structure, and you will find sheepshead. The trick is getting them to bite.

## Lures

Sheepshead can be caught on lures, but you have to work at it. In other words, there are easier ways of catching sheepshead than using lures. Those that are productive, however, are small and exploit a heavy feeding pattern.

## Soft-bodied Jigs

Tiny soft-bodied jigs are useful if you know how to use them. After the chum is in the water, dangle a micro jig with a shredded tail that has been soaked in fish attractant right beside a piling or rock where the sheepshead are

**The author works a pier's pilings for sheepshead with fiddler crabs.**

feeding. Move it back and forth near the structure and bump it often. Sheepshead see this and think it is some sort of bait picking up minuscule food particles. Crappie jigs are great for this. Yellow is a good color.

## Hard-bodied Jigs

These aren't used as much as the soft-bodied because they do not appear as lifelike.

There aren't a lot of other lures that will take sheepshead, since most imitate bait fish and sheepshead don't eat fish.

## Live And Cut Bait

Fill a mesh laundry bag—or #10 can with holes punched in it—with chum and lower it near the structure. The current and wave action will spread the tiny particles of food around and get the sheepshead thinking about eating. A live shrimp, piece of clam or mussel, or small fiddler crab lowered among the feeding sheepshead will produce if you have used the right size hook.

**Getting below the pier may be answer to the sheepshead riddle.**

# Hot Spots

Structure is paramount, and anywhere you find structure with barnacles and other sea life attached, you will find a sheepshead.

**Waiting and hoping.**

## From Piers, Jetties, Wharves, And Bridges

You can tell a good sheepshead structure by the number of sheepshead anglers hanging over the edge. And with the number of piers, jetties, wharves and bridges along the Carolinas' coasts, it is no problem finding one that harbors sheepshead.

Any bridge that has been over the Intracoastal Waterway long enough to get barnacles growing on the pilings is a likely spot. Anchor below or tie up to the bridge and go to it.

## In The Shallows

The lagoons and flats of the Carolinas often have shoals of oyster beds that attract sheepshead. As with reds, you can stalk sheepshead that are feeding on these beds and have a lot of fun doing it.

A slow, cautious approach is required. Sheepshead are suspicious of anything moving in the shallows around them, and will flee if they think a human is near. Polarized sunglasses help in spotting them. When you see sheepshead working an oyster bed, put on a live shrimp and toss it a few yards in front of the fish. Let the fish come to the bait. Dragging it toward the fish could spook them. A small shrimp with a light weight is best. Pieces of shrimp work, too, as do pieces of bloodworms and sandworms.

# Sheepshead Tackle

You won't need specialized tackle for sheepshead, but where and how you are fishing is going to play a role in the rod, reel, and line you select.

## Rods

On the pier you are going to need a little heavier rod than you would use on the flats, wharves, and jetties. This is because you are going to have to winch the sheepshead up onto the pier, and this journey is often quite long. A stout, ultrafast action pier rod will help bring the sheepshead up and keep it out of the pilings where it definitely is going to try to go. All of this applies to bridges, too.

You can get away with a slightly lighter rod with fast action on wharves and jetties. While the pier rod might be 7-feet long, the wharf, shallows, and jetty rod can be a 6-footer. A medium light rating is perfect.

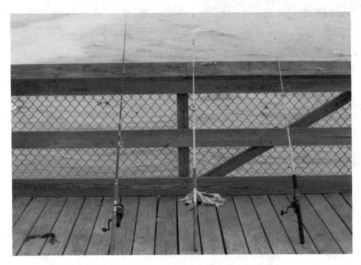

**Medium-sized spinning reels and rods with backbone are called for to catch sheepshead.**

**Pilings covered with barnacles demand abrasion resistant line.**

## Reels

Most sheepshead are fought with spinning reels, and you need not spend a lot of money on one. The same reel you use for seatrout and reds will do for sheepshead. Set your drag a little tighter than normal and you will have less trouble with fish that want to go into the pilings or other structure to break the line.

## Line

Pier line should be heavier than normal, or use one of the braided lines that resist chafes. If you forget that the sheepshead is going to try repeatedly to drag your line over sharp edges you won't be catching many. I wouldn't go any lighter than 10-pound test, and would probably use 15-pound test. I recommend Stren Super Tough for its abrasion resistance.

Waders on the flats can go lighter, but anything under 6-pound test is probably too light. Use line that isn't brightly colored: sheepshead spook at bright line, and when in the shallows you have to take every precaution to keep the fish calm as you approach.

## Hooks

A 2/0 or thereabouts is a good sheepshead hook, generally speaking, but it really depends on the average size of the sheepshead you are after and what kind and size of bait you are using. In any case, a little experimentation will do the trick.

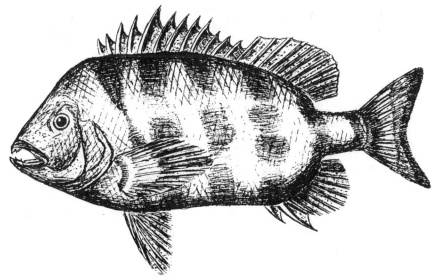

**Sheepshead.**

89

# Catching Crabs

Sheepshead love fiddler crabs and they are easy to catch if you know the secret. You will need a bucket and two boards, each about 5 feet long each.

Head to your local lagoon or other shallows area at low tide and look for exposed mud banks where the fiddlers are sunning and eating. You'll see them scampering around. Dig a hole deep enough to bury the bucket up to the lip and set the bucket in it. Now set the boards in a "V" shape with the bottom of the "V" behind the bucket so that they form walls. You should be looking at a sort of funnel now. Walk several meters away from the opening of the "V," then back toward the trap. The fiddlers will run from you and be funnelled into the bucket as they hit the boards. When you have enough just pick up the bucket with your crabs, and the boards, and head for sheepshead waters.

Sheepshead are so much fun to fight, so finicky, and so delicious that I had better warn you before you go that they are addicting. Catch one, and you will want more.

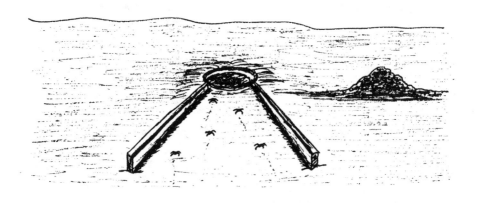

**The 'bucket and boards' crab trap.**

# Chapter 9
# Other Fish Worth A Try

While the species discussed in previous chapters are considered to be the top inshore game fish of the Carolinas, they are by no means the only ones enticing anglers. Here are some of the more popular of the other fish, along with the best times, places and techniques for catching them.

## Striped Bass

Striped bass, known as rockfish here and stripers up north, are a game fish of historical importance. Since the 1600s they have fed and entertained countless Americans from New England to Florida. They have even been introduced to the West Coast (in 1879 and 1882) where they now make up a big part of the Pacific Northwest's saltwater fishery. They have an outstanding reputation as brawlers with delicate, delicious meat.

Rockfish are caught on all sorts of lures, live, and cut bait from spring through fall, with the best action being at the beginning of each season. They can be found in rivers and estuaries as well as off beaches and jetties. Eels, sandworms and bloodworms, finger mullet, and a variety of lures will take them.

The rockfish was nearly wiped out by overfishing and habitat destruction years ago. Today their populations are back from the brink because of hard work and a love for the fish.

**Plenty of so-called lesser game fish inhabit the Carolina surf, such as striped bass, spot, croaker, and pompano. Medium-light spinning tackle can take them all.**

## Pompano

Pompano are a favorite of ultralight tackle surf casters from spring through fall, but late summer is best. These delicious little fish live in the surf and eat sand fleas (mole crabs). The trick to catching them is keeping the bait close to shore where the surf turns to foam. Sift some wet sand where the waves retreat and find some fleas. Put one on a No. 1 hook with a piece of split shot and toss it right into the front of the surf. It won't be long before you feel a tug.

## Atlantic Croaker

Croakers are extremely common in our inshore waters, found from the surf to the rivers, and when played on the lightest possible tackle—an ultralight 5- or 5 1/2-foot rod with 2-pound test—they are fun and scrappy. Try using a yellow, chartreuse, or white crappie jig (chenille body) soaked with Baitmate Shrimp or Saltwater flavor attractant. Tipping the end of the jig with a thin sliver of squid is also highly productive. But croakers also hit clam strips, cut bait fish, and a weirdly wide variety of other baits. Name it, and croakers probably eat it. They taste okay, but are not thought of as food of the gods. They can be caught, however, from spring well into fall.

**Sea mullet and pompano are two pier favorites.**

# Spot

These salt-water panfish are to our inshore waters what bluegills are to inland ponds. Spot fishing is great during the late summer and fall, and they are most often caught in the surf, from piers, and in the Intracoastal Waterway wherever a confluence occurs.

Any worm or piece of worm will catch a spot: you don't have to buy bloodworms or sandworms; just use earthworms. Spots also hit very thin strips of squid, pieces of shrimp and bait fish.

Spots are tasty, and you can get a mess of them in short order. If you go spot fishing, chances are you are going to come home with something. Use ultralight tackle, since they average less than a pound.

# Sea Mullet

Sea mullet, or whiting, are not related to finger mullet or any other true mullet. Caught on pieces of bloodworm or sandworm, and sometimes small pieces of squid and similar baits used for croakers, the sea mullet can go a few pounds and fights well for its size. Try fishing for them at night with a No. 2 hook baited with a piece of bloodworm fished right in the surf. Light tackle is best, and they really put on a good show.

**Estuaries hold croakers and pinfish that can make a kid's day.**

**Getting set for some action at the end of the pier.**

**Pinfish are abundant and fun on ultralight tackle.**

# Pinfish

Pinfish are possibly the most cooperative and reliable little salt-water panfish along the Carolinas' coasts. Dwelling around pilings and other structure, these feisty little guys are great for teaching kids how to fish. They willingly gobble all sorts of cut bait and even tiny jigs doused with fish attractant or tipped with strips of clam, shrimp, or squid.

Ultralight tackle is the best way to catch these fish. You will not need any more than 2-pound test line and a short ultralight rod with a small spinning reel. Pinfish hang beneath every pier and wharf in the Carolinas from spring through fall.

An ultralight spinning rig and some cut bait will produce bucketsful. You can't miss.

# Chapter 10
# Finding Your Niche

With such diverse coastlines, the Carolinas offer myriad places and ways to fish. We have an abundance of piers that afford anglers the chance to catch everything from pinfish to sharks. We have rivers, creeks, sounds and estuaries that hold spotted seatrout, sheepshead, flounder, tarpon, and many other game fish. We have the Intracoastal Waterway that is filled with all sorts of sporting fighters. We have our fabulous beaches that are home to giant drum and mean bluefish. And the waters beyond the beach have cobia, spanish mackerel, and smoker kings.

The problem here is that you have to know the intricacies of each type of place if you want to have success at them all.

## Pier Pressure

Knowing how to work a pier is crucial if you want to catch lots of fish from them. Those who have yet to crack the code walk away frustrated and swear never to return. But those who have learned the secrets of pier fishing have a great deal of fun and take some truly huge fish.

There is much more to successful pier fishing than having the right rods for the species you are after. You know from the previous chapters that the rod you use is dependent on the fish you are trying to catch, but how are you supposed to go lugging these rods around with all the other stuff that goes along with them? Pier carts can be made or bought that handle this chore for you. They have rod holders built into them, and room for your tackle box, bait bucket, cooler, and other items you will want along.

**Pier fishing requires specialized tackle and tactics.**

A seat cushion for the benches or a folding lawn chair (if the pier allows them) is a good idea, as is warm clothing for the cooler seasons. Piers can get downright cold when the wind gets to howling in the spring and fall, and winter pier fishing can freeze you almost solid. Early morning and night fishing during summer can get cooler than you might think, so bring a jacket then as well.

As with all types of fishing in the Carolinas, you will need a hat and sunglasses to suit the season. The South's sun will cook your brain if you let it, and the glare from the water can bring on a merciless headache. Bring sunscreen and lip balm.

A flying gaff (gaff hook on a rope) is needed for bigger fish. Another length of rope is needed for the live bait bucket to float beneath the pier.

Sneakers or other comfortable shoes are mandatory, as you likely will be standing for long periods.

## Surf Action

Surf casters are a hardy breed who will face a bitter north wind for a bull red. Four-wheel drive pickups are popular for getting around the remote stretches of sand that don't have regular roads. Rod holders fastened to the front make it easy to keep gear ready for quick fishing. Insulated rubber boots and hip waders keep the cold surf at bay.

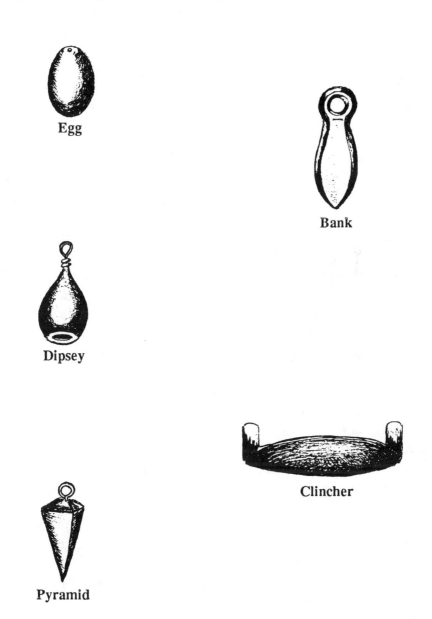

**A variety of sinkers will help you fish different situations.**

The surf casters tackle box is heavy. It is filled with all kinds and sizes of sinkers to handle the various conditions: pyramid, egg, bank, hurricane, clincher, dipsey and split shot. That box also holds different kinds of swivels, bottom rigs, leaders, hooks, spools of line, and more lures than you know what to do with.

The surf caster will have his favorite folding chair along, and sand spikes to hold every rod securely in place. Besides all this, he'll have the warm clothes, sun protection devices, and other accoutrements of the pier angler.

# River, Creek, Estuary, and Sound Fishing

If there is one type of fishing in the Carolinas' inshore waters that requires special attention to detail and a thorough reconnaissance, it is fishing the rivers, creeks, estuaries and sounds. Yes, it is true that you have to do your homework to fish successfully from our piers, beaches, and from boats, but this type of fishing leaves little room for error.

Since you are going to be shorebound for this type of fishing, or wading, and the areas often have tight access (meaning you may not be able to drive along the water looking for the best spot), you will have to be equipped properly. You'll be using one rod more than likely, and often will have to move along the shore by walking or wading. Heavy tackle boxes dragged along behind you are a nuisance, so you should buy a fishing vest like those worn by fly fishers, which is a tackle box for your body. It carries everything you need: lures and cut bait, extra line, sinkers, terminal gear, a flashlight, your lunch, a net, a gaff, clippers, hook removers (hemostats), fish attractant, a camera, sunglasses, lip balm, sun screen, truck keys, gloves, bandages, a small canteen, and so on. Even with all this gear hanging from your body, the vest is quite light and comfortable because its weight is distributed across your shoulders.

Buying one is easy, too. An L.L. Bean, Orvis, or Cabela's fishing catalog is all you need. The vests come in many makes and models, some that even have built-in life preservers.

Waders are also something you'll want to invest in. If you are going to be wading at any time other than summer, get the insulated chest waders so you won't freeze. Polypropylene longjohns worn underneath the waders during cold weather are a godsend. Some models have the boot already attached, while others are stocking-foot types that require separate boots.

Check a topographic map to see how best to access areas that may be new to you. Trying different areas off the beaten path, especially along the Intracoastal Waterway, is fun and often very productive. But while wading

100

**Wading anglers can take trout in a host of locations.**

the Intracoastal beware those big barges and yachts that will throw huge waves your way and suck you out into the channel if you ignore them.

# Boating

With the wide selections available, it can be tough deciding which boat to buy. The best advice I've heard is this: buy the biggest and most versatile boat you can afford.

The better inshore boats are between 19- and 23-feet long with a center console. The outboard is powerful enough to get you to the fish quick, but not a gas hog. The hull is either a deep-vee or modified deep-vee so that you can handle tall water when you need to and have a smooth ride the rest of the time. Such a boat will also have a live well, depth/fish finder, Loran, Global Positioning System (GPS), VHF (marine) radio, trolling rod holders and "rocket launcher" rod holders attached to the t-top for when you are running, ample storage under the front seat cooler and console, fish storage space (usually up by the anchor locker), a trolling motor, two bottom anchors, and a sea anchor.

The manufacturer's name plays a big role in how much your boat will cost. If it says Grady White, Fountain, Ranger, or Albemarle on the hull, sticker

101

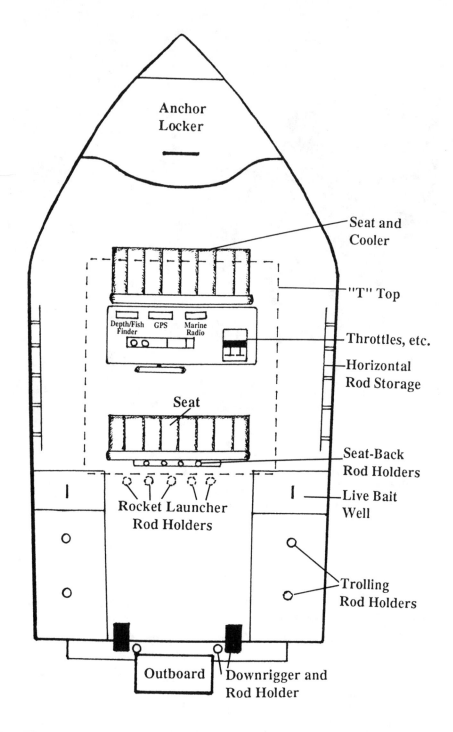

Anchor
Locker

Seat and
Cooler

"T" Top

Depth/Fish
Finder    GPS    Marine
Radio

Throttles, etc.

Horizontal
Rod Storage

Seat

Seat-Back
Rod Holders

Rocket Launcher
Rod Holders

Live Bait
Well

Trolling
Rod Holders

Outboard

Downrigger and
Rod Holder

**How you set up your boat is crucial to success and safety.**

**Downriggers are an important part of the inshore boat.**

shock is almost a guarantee. A Mako costs a little less. Other brand names such as Key West and Cajun are more affordable. Outboard motors are expensive no matter what the make. Force, Mariner, Mercury, Evinrude, Johnson, Suzuki, and Honda are all reliable and easily available. Electric trolling motors by Motor Guide, Mercury, and other trustworthy brands are getting less expensive thanks to new technology

The same thing goes for depth/fish finders. Hummingbird makes some of the best.

Be careful when buying a used boat and motor, and do not buy from someone who is hesitant about putting it in the water. The hull is usually the least of your worries, since the motor and electronics take more of a beating than does the hull.

# Moving and Hauling

How you transport your tackle, rods, and reels is almost a science in and of itself. The wrong tackle box or rod case can cost you big bucks. That is why you must choose very carefully when buying such items.

## Tackle Boxes

The No. 1 name in tackle boxes is of course Plano. Their boxes are tough, reliable, designed with common sense and ingenuity. Coastal Carolina anglers are fond of Plano's roomy Model 9606, which can store several spools of extra line, another reel, loads of lures and terminal gear, and nearly everything else you might need. One step down is the Model 8606, which I really like. I have used mine for years and can't seem to destroy it no matter how hard I try. And Plano's unique StowAway system in boxes such as their Model 1233 makes changing tackle easy.

For a catalog of Plano tackle boxes and rod tubes, write to: Plano Molding Company, 431 E. South St., Plano, IL 60545-1601 (708) 552-8989.

The only other major brand name tackle box maker is Flambeau.

## Rod Tubes

Rod tubes and cases that are airline baggage handler proof are tough to come by. Orvis makes some beauties, or you can try one I use that is made by Boulder Landing. This company makes the Genesis Series rod case that is very rugged and can handle any situation. Innovation was used in designing this case. Contact Boulder Landing Rod Cases, 3728 S. Elm Place, Suite 532, Broken Arrow, OK 74011 (918) 455-3474.

# Chapter 11
# Fish On A Fly

Fly fishing has grown in popularity at an amazing rate in recent years. Yet too many anglers still think that fly fishing is only for mountain-stream trout anglers with lots of money. Nothing could be further from the truth.

So why the sudden remarkable increase in the number of anglers chasing all types of fish with fly rods?

There is no one reason. The hit movie *A River Runs Through It* is partly responsible. Fly fishing clinics also are hot and people are learning that fly fishing not only is easy to learn but that it's a good way to catch fish. And fly fishing tackle is affordable, fun to use, and versatile.

All these factors have made fly fishing a growing phenomenon. And more and more anglers are discovering that almost every species along the Carolinas' coasts can be caught on a fly rod, offering more challenge and fun than fishing by other means. This is something you've got to try.

Start by asking a local fly fisher or tackle shop owner who understands the sport what you need. If you will be spending most of your time for reds, blues, and seatrout, go with an 8 1/2- to 9-foot graphite 8-weight rod. It doesn't have to be a $500 rod, either. St. Croix, L.L. Bean, and other big names make starter rods that are outstanding bargains. Your reel should have a reliable drag and exposed rim for palming, and be designed for the rigors of salt water. Again, no need to buy one that is overly expensive.

Lines are a story unto themselves. Fly lines made by Orvis, Scientific Anglers, and Fenwick are popular because they are of high quality and last a long time with care. Fly lines are classified by taper, weight, and whether they float or sink. Weights run from featherweight 2s to the heavy 12s.

The code on a fly line box is simple to decipher. A code that reads WF-6-F is a weight forward (for better casting the line is slightly heavier toward the front of the line), 6-weight, floating line. An L-10-F/S is a level taper, 10-weight, floating line with a tip that sinks. A DT-7-S is a double taper (a line that can be taken off the reel and reversed), 7-weight, sinking line. Sinking lines come in various rates of sink, too, from slow to fast. An intermediate line is one that sinks slowly.

At the end of a fly line goes the leader and tippet. These are monofilament extensions used to separate the fat fly line from the fly so that casting is more efficient and the fly line doesn't spook the fish. Tippet material is a thinner piece of leader that is used for finer presentations and extending a short leader.

You don't have to learn how to tie your own flies to be a fly fisher. Just get a fly fishing catalog and buy a ready-made selection of salt-water flies, or call the company's rep at the factory and ask for advice. Reading fly fishing magazines and some of the many salt-water fly fishing books on the market will vastly increase your know-how.

Tom Rosenbauer of Orvis, one of the country's premier fly fishing companies, tells me that Orvis is planning to hold salt-water fly fishing clinics in the Carolinas beginning in 1994. He says that with the ever-growing interest in the sport that many fly fishing experts believe this area is going to become the next hot spot for saltwater fly fishing.

# Which Rod For Which Fish

You can handle small reds, blues, and most seatrout on anything from a 5-weight to a 9-weight. Bull reds, bruiser blues, big black drum, and tarpon require from a 10-weight to a 12-weight. Conditions play a role in which weight you use, too. Heavier lines work better in windy conditions and when the current is running strong and you need to get down. Graphite rods in the 9-foot range that have high modulus ratings (are stiffer) can fit the bill for most situations.

A warning about fly fishing: once you learn how to do it and catch your first fighting game fish, you are going to be hooked yourself. You will find that you begin to think long, philosophical thoughts about tarpon, redfish, and bluefish that you never thought before. You'll start ordering fly fishing catalogs and magazines so you can study the art, and you may very well start fly fishing in fresh water, too. Your spinning gear may get dusty.

# Chapter 12
# Saving Our Coastal Environment

Wilderness along the Carolinas' coasts disappeared, for the most part, long ago. The hand of man is everywhere now.

We have tilled the soil for our crops and applied heinous chemicals to kill whatever threatened them. These wash into our waters as agricultural runoff to poison and kill what lives therein. We construct sewage treatment facilities that leak untold tons of toxins into the water. Our boats leak fuel and oil. Factories and mills dump pollutants secretly into wetlands bordering fishing grounds. Commercial fishermen overharvest. Ships toss garbage overboard, and it ends up on our beaches. Wetlands and riparian zones are filled in to make way for strip malls, vacation homes, parking lots, mobile home parks, and highways.

Why do we insist on destroying what we cherish?

## Our Imperiled Wetlands

All of our fishing depends entirely on the state of our wetlands. Sadly, we have done a terrible job of preserving them.

South Carolina has only 23 per cent of its wetlands remaining; North Carolina a mere 16 per cent. Wetlands are sensitive, fragile mechanisms that do much more than provide a home for fish, birds, mollusks, crustaceans, reptiles, amphibians, and mammals. They act as buffers that store and slow the rise of flood waters; some types can actually filter toxic heavy metals, pesticides, coliform bacteria, and chemical pollutants; they help steady shorelines from erosion; they play a role in maintaining water quality by trapping sediments; and they produce life-giving oxygen. But despite all this, many interests in the Carolinas want to destroy wetlands for profit.

# A Special Coastline

The Carolinas are protected from the sea by a unique string of barrier islands and their ecosystems. These are extremely precarious environments that are subject not only to the whims of nature, but the malice of man. The islands we know as Hatteras, Ocracoke, Portsmouth, Kiawah, Fripp, Bull and their like play a pivotal role in the health of the wetlands that surround them. Development along such shores has laid waste to millions of acres of wetlands that will never be recovered. People build vacation houses on stilts over the surf, and they wonder why they fall into the sea when a storm passes. Erosion caused by their driveways and the roads that lead to them shifts the course of nature, not only killing fish but keeping fish from being born because their wetland nurseries are gone.

So what are we doing to stop this?

# Acts

The Coastal Barrier Improvement Act of 1990 has helped by limiting federal assistance meant for developers who want to put houses, roads, malls, and parking lots on barrier islands. The Coastal Barrier Resource System is made up of 1.25-million acres of coastline that falls under this act, but unfortunately politicians have found loopholes for constituents who donate large sums to their reelection campaigns. As anglers we must keep a close eye on who our elected representatives accept campaign funds from in exchange for political favors that allow them to get by the law.

The North American Wetlands Conservation Act, also enacted in 1990, allocates as much as $26 million every year for the purchase and protection of wetlands, and some in the Carolinas are being preserved as a result.

# The Creek, Stream, and Estuary Connection

There is no ecosystem that is entirely independent: they all rely on each other to one degree or another. This means that what happens in one can adversely affect what happens in another many miles away. A spill from a sewage treatment facility in the upper New River can toxify or kill life along the river all the way to the sea.

**A sign of the times.**

Pesticides that run off a farm along the Salkehatchie River can find their way down to the Combahee and into St. Helena Sound. Garbage tossed overboard from passing ships washes into our estuaries and fouls fishing grounds and bird nesting sites. Tires dumped in the shallows will remain there for decades.

Estuaries, creeks, and streams have long been the dumping grounds of a huge array of polluters. Poisons such as DDT, PCBs (polychlorinated biphenyls), plastics, petroleum hydrocarbons, copper, zinc, lead, cadmium, and arsenic all lurk in the waters where we fish—and end up in the fish we eat. Shellfish are more toxic than fin fish in most cases, because they stay in one place and continually siphon water that holds toxins, which are transferred to

**Garbage can be seen in all our waters at low tide.**

their tissue. Consequently, vast areas of oyster and clam beds have been closed, but pirate watermen take countless bushels of the shellfish from them under night skies for sale to markets and restaurants. The results can be tragic.

When we think of polluters we usually envision belching factories and mills, but the primary nonpoint source of stream pollution comes from agriculture. More than 60 per cent of our streams are affected by toxins that leave the farm as runoff. No other source is anywhere near this great.

The Carolinas are an agrarian region that produces a wide array of crops, from corn to soybeans. But we must strive to find a way for farmers to get away from the use of deadly chemicals to increase crop yield. The farmers are not fully to blame for this situation, of course, because they use what is available. What we must do is get better products for use on the farm so that cheap grains and vegetables don't end up killing our fish.

The Carolinas have also had a tough time with municipal sewage making its way downstream to damage coastal waters. Many towns and cities have antiquated treatment facilities that are a never-ending source of such serious pollutants as coliform bacteria.

Heavy development and new construction are also dire threats along the coasts, where population is increasing rapidly. We clearly have our work cut out for us if we expect to save any fish for our children.

## The Money

State and local governments of the Carolinas have never been greatly concerned about the environment. North Carolina spends only about 1per cent of its money on protecting the environment, and it releases more than 60 thousand tons of pollutants every year. South Carolina has only a slightly better record, spending about 1.2 per cent, while releasing approximately 42 thousand tons of pollutants.

One would expect that two states with such a vested interest in fisheries would see to it that our resources are protected, but that just isn't happening.

## Commercial Interests

It is easy to lay much blame for declining fish populations on commercial fishermen, as some sport anglers are prone to do, but we can't throw it all on their shoulders, either. Yes, overharvesting is a serious problem today as it has always been. Sport fishermen accuse gill netters of setting nets in places that wipe out entire runs of seatrout and other fish, but the netters deny it. Shrimpers have been known to destroy bottom terrain by dragging nets too low for too long, and they have been accused of taking too many shrimp. The overharvesting of shrimp obviously leads to declines in game fish populations because fish feed on shrimp.

This is another Catch-22 situation: we, the consumers, demand more fish at the market for less money. To get this the commercial fishermen fish longer and harder, wrecking the populations and the habitat. Pollution's awful toll adds to the mayhem. We have brought this situation on ourselves, and only we can fix it.

## Victims

The coastal Carolinas are home to many endangered species. including the alligator and several sea turtles. Although the alligator is a genuine success story, having been brought back from the brink of extinction, the sea turtles that lay their eggs in our sand are another story. Habitat destruction, nets, and

Courtesy of US Marine Corps

**A sea turtle makes her way back to sea from a nest site.**

intrusion by people are the three primary reasons sea turtles are in trouble along our coast.

If you see someone tampering with a turtle nesting site, stop them. These animals act as a barometer and tell us about the condition of our coastal areas. When they decline, we know that we are not taking care of what is ours.

We can't expect to have tomorrow what we killed in years past, but we can all make a difference if we use common sense. Catch-and-release fishing is an ethic that deserves special attention from us. If you don't need that fish, let it go as a hedge for tomorrow. Elect politicians that will protect our environment, or send them packing. Form action groups to address local problems, which are easier to solve at home than at the state capital. An appendix listing environmental organizations with which you may want to get involved appears at the back of this book.

# Chapter 13
# Where The Fish Are

So far we have learned life histories of the most popular inshore game fish along the Carolinas' coasts, their favorite habitats, and how you can catch them. Now it's time to name some places where you're apt to have some luck.

We'll start up north and work our way down the coast, first in general terms, then with more specifics.

## North Carolina
### Currituck Sound

Currituck Sound is accessible from the many little communities lining it both on the mainland and barrier island side, including Knotts Island, Duck, Waterlily, and Poplar Branch. This sound has red drum, spotted seatrout and flounder in its many nooks and crannies.

### Albemarle Sound

With an expensive line of fishing boats named after it, you would think that Albemarle Sound would have good fishing, and it does. Mid-summer tarpon are available, as are trout, flounder, and drum. Fish the confluences and creeks. Try where the Alligator, Chowan, Perquimans, and Little Rivers join the sound, along with Batchelor Bay, Bull Bay, and all the points.

## Kill Devil Hills & Nags Head Area

Out on the banks, these two fishing jump-off spots are popular because a lot of fish are caught near them. On the ocean side you have great drum and bluefish angling, while on the sound side you have flounder, trout, tarpon, and other game fish.

## Pamlico Sound

The largest sound in the Carolinas, Pamlico is rich with tradition and fish. From Cedar Island to Wanchese you can catch tarpon, croakers, sea mullet, flounder, red and black drum, spotted seatrout, gray trout, blues, and many other fish. Focus on the points and confluences where the Neuse and Pamlico Rivers merge with the sound. Good points are Point of March, Long Shoal, Bluff, Sandy, Stumpy, and Bay.

## Cape Hatteras

Such a famous name means great fishing. From renowned Oregon Inlet in the north to Hatteras Inlet in the south, big fish cruise the beaches and cuts. Huge red drum, black drum, and bluefish are the primary draw, but you'll also find great king mackerel, spanish mackerel, flounder, cobia, and little tunny inshore. A trip to Hatteras is an experience you won't soon forget.

## Ocracoke Island

This 16-mile-long island has fishing equivalent to Hatteras. Hit the 59, 68, and 72 Ramps, Ocracoke Inlet, Wallace Channel, and Vera Cruz Shoal.

## Portsmouth Island

Portsmouth Island offers remote fishing and fast action for those who take the trouble to get to it. From the village of Atlantic you have to take Capt. Morris' ferry over to Portsmouth (919-225-4261). Get a vehicle permit from the National Park Service (PO Box 690, Beaufort, NC 28516) before you try to get on the ferry. You can rent cabins from the NPS from $40-$120 per night. Take everything you will need. There are no stores.

## Core Banks

This barrier island makes up the lowermost island of the Cape Lookout National Seashore, and fishing its inshore waters is wonderful for big drum, flounder, and a variety of other game fish.

## Morehead City

Morehead City is a thriving seaport that is home to a large sportfishing fleet and numerous mackerel, marlin, and seatrout tournaments. From Morehead you can easily fish all of the Bogue Banks from Emerald Isle to Atlantic Beach, Bogue Sound, and the Shackleford Banks. The bridge between Radio Island and Morehead City (U.S. Highway 70) is a trout hot spot. Cobia and mackerel are common at the channel mouth off Fort Macon, across the sound from Morehead City. Hit the buoys there hard. The nearby rock jetty harbors sheepshead and other species.

## White Oak River

A classic Carolina coastal river, the White Oak comes out of Wolf Swamp and empties into the Atlantic at the quaint village of Swansboro. Seatrout and flounder are big here. Try around the N.C. Highway 24 bridge and the flats behind it. If you are hungry, try Yana's Restaurant in the village for the best grub this side of Raleigh.

## New River Inlet

You'll always see plenty of anglers around this inlet and up the river to Snead's Ferry. The bridges at Snead's Ferry hold big sheepshead, and the better holes have gigantic trout that go 10 pounds and more. The inlet is good for spanish, blues, flounder, and kings a little farther out. The summer surf is rich with pompano.

## Lower Onslow Bay

This is the area from the New River Inlet down to Cape Fear. All the piers jutting into the Atlantic here indicate that the fish are here. Some of the hottest king and spanish mackerel fishing is found along this strip. The inlets—New Topsail, Rich, Mason, and Corncake—are all productive.

## Upper Long Bay

From Fort Caswell and Bald Head Island south to Tubbs Inlet, try the Shallotte and Lockwoods Folly Inlets for flounder and trout.

# South Carolina
## The Grand Strand
The Grand Strand stretches from North Myrtle Beach to North Island, and flounder, bluefish, sea mullet, pompano, spot, mackerel, and trout can be caught all along it. Where you see boats milling around off the piers you will find fish.

## Santee Rivers Area
The North and South Santee Rivers join the Atlantic at Cedar Island. Drum, trout and mackerel fishing is good here. Hector Reef off Georgetown gives up many big kings.

## Bulls Bay
This bay separates Cape Romain from Bull Island and is home to drum, sea mullet, pompano, spanish, kings, and trout. Work the Intracoastal at the back of the bay for gray trout and specks.

## Charleston
Charleston is not only scenic and historic, it also offers some fine inshore fishing. Try the creek mouths for drum and trout, and blues feed in the heavy current along the jetty on the south side of Charleston Harbor. Dewees and Stono Inlets always have anglers working them.

## St. Helena Sound Area
Edisto Island south to Hunting Island is the St. Helena Sound area, and this is a hot region for flounder and mackerel. Seatrout frequent all the creeks mouths and estuaries of the Combahee River region.

## Port Royal Sound
Bordering the infamous Marine Corps Recruit Depot on Parris Island, Port Royal Sound is often swarming with anglers trying for flounder, gator trout, drum, and sharks. Fishing for mackerel is good just offshore. Do not assist any AWOL Marine recruits you see trying to swim to England.

## Hilton Head

This beautiful resort island is well known for giving up door mat flounder and hefty seatrout, as well as giant king mackerel and no small amount of respectable spanish. Get back in the creeks for croaker and gray trout, and specks.

# Specific Spots
# North Carolina
## Currituck Beach to Kitty Hawk Region

Specks, red and black drum, flounder, sea mullet, blues and croaker are all caught regularly from the Virginia line to Kitty Hawk. Look for rocks, wrecks, drop-offs and other structure along the beach at low tide. Try the wreck out from Fresh Pond Hill, the wreck down the beach from Whale Head Hill, and the one just above the Dare County line.

## Kitty Hawk to North Point/Roanoke Sound and Croatan Sound

Wrecks, spoil areas, and rocks are more common along the beach in this area, and it is more accessible, which of course means more people fish thereabouts. Following the fish and birds is one of the best ways to find the fish here, rather than focusing on one spot. The waters off the piers are often rich in game fish and are good places to start if no birds or groups of anglers are working the area.

The sounds are a different story. Here you often can find fish holding or moving through certain areas. Look for specks in Spencer Creek, off Sand Point, between Mann's Harbor and Weir Point on Roanoke Island, up into Broad Creek, above Pond Island, and all through the Oregon Inlet region. Blues like working the channels, and some great drum action is found in Oregon Inlet, and the sandy bottom areas between U.S. Highway 64/264 and Oregon Inlet hold some huge doormat flounder. Where Croatan Sound melds with Pamlico Sound is an area known for good spanish mackerel and bluefish angling. If it's cobia you seek, put out a chum line right off Oregon Inlet. Second Slough and State Reef AR-160 (Oregon Inlet) are outstanding king mackerel spots.

## Albemarle Sound

Tarpon cruise all the waters of Albemarle Sound, but focus your attention on cuts that have a lot of forage shooting through them. Don't be afraid to get in close to shore, but be cautious of the many submerged obstructions. From Dewey Pier across to Wade Point is frequently productive. This area also holds loads of croakers, and you can really have fun with the kids and ultralight spinning rigs here. Flounder are often thick right off of Pledger Landing.

Working the grass banks around Haulover Point at the tip of the Alligator River National Wildlife Refuge for seatrout and puppy drum often turns up trout in the 2- to 5-pound range and drum around 18-inches or so, which is the minimum legal length limit in North Carolina as of this writing. Albemarle Sound also has some of the hottest rockfish (striped bass) fishing in North Carolina. Two of the best areas in spring and fall are off Durant Island between Sound Point and Ned Bees Point, and throughout the mouth of the North River. Expect other rockfish fanatics, as these are popular spots.

## Kill Devil Hills Region

Surf fishermen and inshore charter boat captains who use light tackle favor this region because blues, specks, rockfish, and flounder all swarm along the beach. Sometimes there can be almost too many anglers along the beach, but if you get there early when the blues and stripers are running strong, you can get a spot.

## Pamlico Sound

The mouth of Stump Point Bay has a lot of debris along the bottom that holds gray trout, specks, loads of croakers, and smallish blues from time to time. Drift across the mouth between Drain Point and Wild Boar Point. Directly out from Sandy Point is a large area with bottom variances that hold both specks and gray trout. Fish a live shrimp or fat finger mullet in these holes.

Guides working this area know that big trout hang out between Pains Bay and Pingleton Point. Spanish mackerel prowl southeast of Pingleton Shoal.

The shores of Gull Rock Wildlife Management Area are good speck grounds, and Gull Rocks off Bensons Point hold rockfish.

Puppy drum, specks, and gray trout are favorite targets in just about every creek mouth that empties into Pamlico Sound. Juniper Bay, the Swan Quarter Narrows between Marsh Island and Great Island, Swan Quarter Bay, Rose Bay, and Deep Cove are all likely hot spots.

As you head up the Pamlico River, try the shallow water off any point for flounder, specks, puppy drum, and gray trout, as well as croakers. Get in tight for the flounder. The mouth of tiny Lee Creek is a great spot, as is the Pungo River confluence.

To the north of Clam Shoal (and Bird Islands) is good puppy drum territory. Anglers seeking spanish and blues hunt northwest of Shark Shoal and Oliver Reef.

## Hatteras

Hatteras Island and its famed cape have drawn anglers from afar for hundreds of years, and the fishing is still great.

From Oregon Inlet southward you will find all manner of inshore gamefish. Blues, rockfish, speckled trout, spanish and kings, flounder, sea mullet, puppy drum and huge bulls, all roam these waters. To list good spots would be futile, because the fish usually keep moving along the beach. Look for rocks and cuts at low tide, and watch the birds. When menhaden are running, look for oily slicks that offer the possibility of blues and rockfish.

## Neuse River

The Neuse is known for nice puppy drum, which concentrate in the creek mouths and cuts along the flats. Try Spring, Long, Swan, Riggs, and Ball Creeks, using a Beetlespin or chunk of fresh mullet. MirrOlures twitched a foot off the grass banks should attract some specks. Large trout can be found in the drop-offs in Jones Bay.

Flounder anglers drift mullet chunks and clam strips in the small bays around Oriental. This is good croaker country, too.

From Hancock Creek to Great Neck you can find good puppy drum action, both from the banks and in the creek mouths. Courts Creek, Adams Creek at the Back Creek confluence, and Cahoogue Creek are all hot.

## Ocracoke Island

Huge shallows line the back side of Ocracoke, and these should be tried for drum and trout. Channel cuts here sometimes hold black drum. Wallace Channel offers outstanding trout fishing. The surf here often yields big bull, red drum and some giant blacks. This region also has many types of structure that hold big cobia, including pilings, wrecks, rock piles, and platforms. All should be worked. Try fishing a live crab on the bottom of Hatteras Inlet for tarpon.

## Core Banks

The waters around these islands are known for good puppy drum and trout fishing. Giggers also take many large flounder in the shallows at night. Mullet are easy to find here, so bring a cast net to catch your own bait. Wading is productive in these tight spots, but go slow so that you don't spook the nervous drum and specks. Try Drum Inlet, around Dump Island, for its namesake catch. Barry Bay, Cedar Island Bay, Nelson Bay, and Great Island Bay are good speck spots.

## Morehead City Region

Morehead City is one of coastal North Carolina's busiest fishing centers. More game fish probably are caught hereabouts than at any other area on the mainland. The area offers numerous charter boats, several head boats, plenty of bait and tackle shops, piers, surf fishing and bridge fishing.

The Atlantic Beach Causeway bridge is a well known cobia hot spot. Jumbo shrimp, menhaden, mullet, crabs, and other cobia favorites tossed near the pilings and fished at various depths could bring the cobia calling. Don't go too light in here, since they will often wrap your line around something. Sheepshead can be found here, too, as well as around the railroad trestle between Morehead City and Beaufort. The many docks and small piers in this area all harbor sheepshead. Try Aaron's Discount Bait & Tackle on the causeway in Atlantic Beach if you need live fiddlers.

The winter of 1993-94 saw dredging going on in the Morehead City channel. I seriously doubt if this was necessary, since I haven't heard of any Navy ships having trouble navigating the channel. The dredging has caused major sand shifting that has radically changed the face of the beaches at the mouth of the channel. The Fort Macon rock jetty was nearly covered with sand early in 1994, which could greatly affect fishing there.

This area has many shoals, grassy islands, cuts, creeks, tiny lagoons, and backwaters that demand experience in fishing them. If you are new to it, there are three ways to fish it: hire a charter, ask help from a bait and tackle shop operator, or follow the other anglers. Navigational charts will be a big help if you decide to tackle it alone.

From Morehead City, it is only a short run to Shackleford Banks and Cape Lookout, where puppy drum, flounder, blues, and specks are good bets.

Bogue Banks from Fort Macon to Bogue Inlet also is a good area for a wide variety of fish, including puppy drum, flounder, spanish, sea mullet, cobia, specks, gray trout, hogfish, spot, croaker, pompano and many others. The

Intracoastal Waterway is fished heavily in this area for specks, and some dandies are taken.

Charter Capt. Joe Shute recommends that puppy drum anglers try the North River between Harkers Island and Beaufort, and the water between the Haystacks and the Morehead high rise bridge.

## Bogue Inlet to New River Inlet

Flounder, puppy drum, and specks are the three most popular fish here and they are especially plentiful around the bridge on N.C. Highway 24 at Swansboro. The flats and creeks upriver from the bridge can be waded at low tide, but be sure to watch the rising tide. Countless grassy banks here hold lots of fish.

A maze of grassy islands, creeks, and estuaries lies between Swansboro and Camp Lejeune. Pole a skiff quietly through this area and you should be able to land drum flounder and specks. The nearby Intracoastal Water way should yield similar results. I have even taken spanish mackerel from the waterway here. Bear Inlet and the Shacklefoot Channel, and Browns Inlet and the Banks Channel, are local favorites. Special tip: Banks Channel just inside Browns Inlet is especially hot for trout.

The swing bridge at Onslow Beach is popular with light tackle anglers looking for trout and flounder. Try Freeman's Creek, too.

New River, from the mouth to Sneads Ferry, draws hoards of anglers. Stones Bay has deep trout holes, as does Ellis Cove, and the old Sneads Ferry bridge has been seeing some big sheepshead caught.

The current really rips at New River Inlet, and this brings in the specks. The open water just beyond the inlet is a good spanish area.

## New River Inlet to Wrightsville Beach

Starting at the bridge on N.C. Highway 210, the warren of meandering creeks, channels, cuts, and sloughs that line the Intracoastal Waterway draw many hunting fish as well as eager anglers. A canoe or skiff is a great way to navigate these waters. Toss grubs, MirrOlures, spinnerbaits, shrimp, and other Carolina favorites for specks, flounder, croaker, gray trout, puppy drum, spot, pinfish, tarpon, and blues. Stump Sound, Alligator Bay, Virginia Creek, Waters Bay, New Topsail Inlet, Old Topsail Inlet, Nixon Channel, and many other spots are likely to hold fish. Rich Inlet is a heavy favorite.

The area from Surf City to Topsail Beach is known for good flounder fishing in the surf, and tarpon are taken on the piers every summer. Spanish mackerel are a pier favorite, as are blues and spots. Mason Inlet, Masonboro Inlet (south of the Coast Guard Station), Howe Creek, and Hewletts Creek usually are productive.

### Wrightsville Beach to Smith Island

Some fine black drum fishing can be had along these beaches. Find a rocky bottom or a shell bed and go to it. Flounder are here as well, as are specks, grays, pompano, croakers, spot, and lots of sea mullet.

Myrtle Grove Sound has Dick Bay, John Creek, Everett Creek and other highly localized hot spots, and be sure to hit Whiskey Creek.

The surf zone south of Carolina Beach Inlet has wrecks and rocks that hold big blues and drum.

Sheepshead Rock is not called that for nothing. Situated just offshore between Fort Fisher and New Inlet, it is a haven for many types of fish. Some huge king mackerel are taken here every year, as are many spanish.

On the inside, try anywhere between Smith Island and Masonboro State Park.

### Oak Island to Little River Inlet

This southernmost stretch of North Carolina surf holds a few wrecks— some exposed, others not—where spanish mackerel can be taken right from the beach. Tom McGlammery Reef lies south of Long Beach, and is known for mackerel fishing.

Lockwoods Folly Inlet has plenty of structure to fish, too, with drum, blues, trout, and flounder all being local favorites. Shallotte Inlet, Tubbs Inlet, and Mad Inlet are all trout locales.

# South Carolina
## Little River Inlet to Murphy Island

Known as the Grand Strand, the section of beach between the Little River Inlet and North island is a tourist magnet. But many of these tourists also like to try a little fishing when the surf is not crowded with people, and they are frequently rewarded. Spanish mackerel, puppy drum, trout, black drum, tarpon, spot, croaker, pompano, cobia, and flounder are all taken from the surf and piers along the Grand Strand. Boaters have good success just offshore, especially at North Inlet, the water between the North Jetty and Cat Island, and Murrell's Inlet. A lot of water moves to and fro here, which draws many game fish. Where the Santee River empties into the Atlantic (South Island, Santee Point, Cedar Island, and Murphy Island), blues work the currents for menhaden and other forage fish.

## Murphy Island to Charleston

The many smaller islands between McClellanville and Cape Island offer outstanding puppy drum and trout action, along with good flounder fishing in the sandy areas. Bulls Bay above Bull Island sees tarpon in the summer, and excellent puppy drum and trout close to shore. King mackerel cruise the mouth of the bay and occasionally get in close, but for the most part they stay a few miles out. You stand a good chance of running into spanish mackerel here, though.

The myriad backwaters of the Cape Romain National Wildlife Refuge are home to croakers in the deeper cuts, flounder in the shallow sandy areas, specks and puppy drum in the creeks and estuaries, and mackerel just offshore. Tarpon are common sights rolling on the surface in this region.

## Charleston to Savannah River

This section is as complicated as the Morehead City region in North Carolina. Riddled with creeks, rivers, coves, flats, and channels, it draws many anglers looking for many types of fishing.

King and spanish mackerel lure them offshore. The running tides pull them to creek mouths where blues and specks come in close.

The Royal, Edisto, Combahee and other coastal rivers offer them puppy drum and tarpon. The Intracoastal Waterway between Morgan Island and Port Royal Sound is one of their favorite spots, consistently yielding drum, trout, flounder and other fish.

# Appendix A

# Carolina Piers

Piers come and go along the Carolinas' coasts. Fires claim some, and hurricanes such as Hugo in 1989 lay waste to others. Some fall victim to bad management and bad luck, and go out of business. The following piers, listed north to south, were open to the public in the spring of 1994. Other piers exist, but some are damaged and temporarily closed, or out of business, others are undergoing changes in ownership, and a few have gone private.

# North Carolina

### Kitty Hawk Fishing Pier
Mile Post 2, PO Box 428, Kitty Hawk, NC 27949 (919) 261-2772.

A 125-pound tarpon was caught from this pier.
Length: 714 feet. Open April 1-November 25. King fishing allowed. No shark fishing. Bait and tackle shop. Restaurant.

### Avalon Fishing Pier
Mile Post 6, Rt. 12, Kill Devil Hills, NC 27948 (919) 441-7494.

Robert Neuman (no relation to the author) caught an 86-pound cobia from this pier in 1989 and B.C. Smith landed a 40-pound sailfish here in 1990
Length: 708 feet. Open mid-March-November. King fishing allowed. No shark fishing. Bait and tackle shop. Rental gear. Snack bar.

### Nags Head Pier
Mile Post 11, Nags Head, NC 27959 (919) 441-5141.

Length: 750 feet. Open mid-March-December 3. King fishing allowed. No shark fishing. Bait & tackle shop. Rental gear. Restaurant. Arcade. Rooms.

## Jennette's Fishing Pier
PO Box 756, Nags Head, NC 27959 (919) 441-6116.

A 750-pound tiger shark was caught here by Rick Ayers in 1986. This pier, built in 1932, was refurbished in 1993.

Length: 707 feet. Open March-November. King and shark fishing allowed. Bait and tackle shop. Restaurant planned for 1995. Cottages.

## Outer Banks Pier
Mile Post 18 1/2, Nags Head, NC 27959 (919) 441-5028.

Length: 650 feet. April-December. King fishing allowed. No shark fishing. Bait & tackle shop. Grill.

## Hatteras Island Pier
Rodanthe, NC 27968 (919) 987-2323.

Length: 600 feet. Open April-December. King fishing allowed. No shark fishing. Bait and tackle shop. Rental gear. Restaurant. Snack bar. Motel with efficiencies. Cottages.

## Avon Pier
PO Box 583, Avon, NC 27915 (919) 995-5480.

Length: 714 feet. Open March 15-December 1. King and shark fishing allowed. Bait and tackle shop. Restaurant.

## Cape Hatteras Pier
Frisco, NC 27936 (919) 986-2533.

This pier is known for tarpon fishing, and many are taken here.

Length 500 feet. Open Easter-Thanksgiving weekend. King fishing allowed. No shark fishing. Bait and tackle shop. Rental gear. Snack bar.

## Triple S Pier
PO Box 306, Atlantic Beach, NC 28512 (919) 726-4170.

Jack Long caught a 105-amberjack from this pier.

Length: 1,000 feet. Open March-November. No king or shark fishing. Bait and tackle shop. Restaurant. Campground.

## Oceanana Fishing Pier

PO Box 250, 700 E. Fort Macon Rd., Atlantic Beach, NC 28512
(919) 726-0863.

Dave Meyers caught a 63-pound cobia here, and Ida Wheeler caught a 43-pound king.

Length: 950 feet. Open mid-March-November. King fishing allowed. No shark fishing. Bait and tackle shop. Grill. Motel. Free fishing for motel guests.

## Sportsman's Pier

500 Money Island Dr., PO Drawer 820, Atlantic Beach, NC 28512
(910) 726-3176.

Walt Corder took an 86-pound cobia in 1982; Joe Squires caught an 83-pound cobia in 1988; and a 64-pound amberjack was caught in 1991 by Bill Mercep. Big tarpon are caught and released here each summer.

Length: 1,150 feet. Open year-round. King fishing Monday-Friday with pier permit. No shark fishing. Bait & tackle shop. Rental gear. Restaurant. Convenience store.

## Iron Steamer

PO Box 187, Atlantic Beach, NC (919) 247-4213.

An 86 1/2-pound tarpon was caught here by Don Blair in 1986; in 1993 Buford Quillen landed a 6-pound 13-ounce spanish, Joey Norris a 5-pound 6-ounce flounder, and Chris Elliott a 10-pound 15-ounce sheepshead.

Length: 750 feet. Open Easter-Thanksgiving. No king or shark fishing. Bait and tackle shop. Rental gear. Grill. Deli. Motel.

## Indian Beach Pier

Morehead City, NC 28557 (919) 247-3411.

Length 710 feet. Open April-Thanksgiving weekend. King fishing allowed. No shark fishing. Bait and tackle shop. Grill. Campground.

## Emerald Isle Pier

PO Box 4807, Emerald Isle, NC 28594 (919) 354-3274.

A record tarpon was taken from this pier.

Length: 900 feet. Open April-November. King fishing allowed. No shark fishing. Bait & tackle shop. Rental gear. Grill.

**Bogue Inlet Pier**
PO Box 4003, Bogue Inlet Dr., Emerald Isle, NC 28594
(919) 354-2919.

In 1993, Bob Stewardson caught a 41 1/2-pound king on this pier, which was damaged by Hurricane Diana in 1984 but has since been restored.
Length 990 feet. Open mid-March-November. King fishing allowed. No shark fishing. Bait and tackle shop.

**Riseley Pier**
Camp Lejeune, NC 28542 (910) 451-7154.

Length 310 feet. Open year-round. King and shark fishing allowed. Bait and tackle shop. Snack bar.

**Ocean City Pier**
PO Box 2220, Surf City, NC 28445 (910) 328-5701.

Known for exceptional catches of seatrout because of the sloughs alongside it, this pier was damaged by a March storm in 1993, but has been rebuilt and strengthened with 75 new pilings.
Length: 850 feet. Open March-November. King and shark fishing allowed. Bait and tackle shop. Rental gear. Restaurant. Golf cart for taking elderly or infirm from car to pier.

**Scotch Bonnet Pier**
Highway 210, North Topsail Beach, NC 28445 (910) 328-4261.

Length: 1,000 feet. Open March-November. King fishing allowed. No shark fishing. Bait and tackle shop. Rental gear. Restaurant. Campground.

**Barnacle Bill's Pier**
Surf City, NC 28445 (910) 328-3661.

Length: 956 feet. Open year-round. King fishing allowed. No shark fishing. Bait & tackle shop. Restaurant.

**Surf City Pier**
Route 210 (at Route 50), Surf City, NC 28445 (910) 328-3521.

Length: 900 feet. Open April-November. King and shark fishing allowed. Bait and tackle shop. Grill.

## Jolly Roger Pier

State Route 50, Surf City, NC 28445 (910) 328-4616 or 1-800-633-3196.

Length 980 feet. Open mid-March-early December. King fishing allowed. No shark fishing. Bait and tackle shop. Restaurant.

## Johnny Mercer's Pier

East Salisbury St., Wrightsville Beach, NC 28480 (910) 256-2743.

Length 750 feet. Open year-round. King fishing allowed. No shark fishing. Bait and tackle shop. Gift shop. Motel.

## Carolina Beach Fishing Pier

U.S. 421, Carolina Beach, NC 28428 (910) 458-5518.

This pier is noted for sheepshead fishing because of the rocky bottom.
Length: 400 feet. Open April-November. King fishing allowed. No shark fishing. Bait and tackle shop. Restaurant.

## Kure Beach Pier

U.S. 421, Kure Beach, NC 28449 (910) 458-5524.

Some nice black drum have been taken from this pier.
Length: 711 feet. Open April-November. King and shark fishing allowed. Bait and tackle shop. Restaurants nearby.

## Yaupon Beach Pier

Yaupon Beach, NC 28461 (910) 278-5962.

This pier was demolished by Hurricane Hugo in 1989 and has been completely rebuilt. It has two "Ts" for added fishing space.
Length 968 feet. Open year-round. King fishing allowed. No shark fishing. Bait and tackle shop. Grill. Restaurant. Lounge.

## Ocean Crest Pier

Long Beach, NC 28461 (910) 278-3333.

Length: 1,000 feet. Open year-round. King fishing allowed. No shark fishing. Bait and tackle shop. Restaurant. Arcade. Motel.

## Long Beach Pier
2729 West Beach Dr., Long Beach, NC  28465 (910) 278-5962.

This pier is famous for king fishing. Here Kathy Davis caught a record king for 16-pound test line: 53 pounds, 8 ounces. In 1977, 37 kings were caught in one day, 242 in a single week. Every summer 300-400 kings are taken here. The pier was rebuilt and lengthened after being wrecked by Hurricane Hugo.

Length: 1,012 feet. Open March-mid-December. King fishing allowed. No shark fishing. Bait and tackle shop. Repair service. Rental gear. Grill. Convenience store. Arcade. Motel.

## Holden Beach Pier
Holden Beach, NC  28462 (910) 842-6483.

Half of this pier was lost to Hurricane Hugo, but it has been fully restored.

Length 900 feet. Open year-round. King and shark fishing allowed. Bait and tackle shop. Rental gear. Grill. Arcade. Campground. Apartments.

## Ocean Isle Pier
Ocean Isle, NC  28549 (910) 579-1270.

Length: 900 feet. Open March-November. King fishing allowed. No shark fishing. Bait & tackle shop. Grill.

# South Carolina

## Cherry Grove Pier
34th Avenue (North), E. Cherry Grove Beach, SC  29582
(803) 249-1625.

This pier is double-decked on the end, which also sports a gazebo.

Length: 985 feet. Open March-Sunday after Thanksgiving. King fishing allowed. No shark fishing. Bait and tackle shop. Restaurant. Arcade.

## Springmaid Pier

South Ocean Beach Blvd., Myrtle Beach, SC 29577 (803) 238-5212.

A record 11-pound spanish was taken from this pier, along with a 49-pound king and a 107-pound tarpon. Heavily damaged by Hurricane Hugo, it has been restored with a 128-wide "T" at the end.

Length: 1,260 feet. Open year-round. King fishing allowed. No shark fishing. Bait and tackle shop. Rental gear. Snack bar.

## Myrtle Beach State Park Fishing Pier

Myrtle Beach State Park, Highway 17 South, Myrtle Beach, SC 29577 (803) 238-0107.

Length: 700 feet. Open year-round. King fishing allowed. No shark fishing. Bait and tackle shop. Snack bar.

## Surfside Pier

PO Box 14489, Surfside Beach, SC 29587 (803) 238-0121.

This pier, which was rebuilt in 1993, gets wider as it goes. Sixteen feet wide at the beach, it expands to 24 feet, then to 35 feet as it reaches out to sea. A 51-pound 4-ounce king was landed here in 1987.

Length 810 feet. Open March-Christmas. King fishing allowed. No shark fishing. Bait and tackle shop. Restaurant. Snack bar. Gift shop.

## The Pier at Garden City

110 Waccamaw Dr. South, Garden City Beach, SC 29576 (803) 651-9700.

Formerly called Kingfisher, this pier was rebuilt in 1991 after falling to Hurricane Hugo.

Length: 660 feet. Open year-round. King fishing limited to two weeks of annual King Mackerel Rodeo. No shark fishing. Bait and tackle shop. Rental gear. Grill. Gift shop.

## Crosby's Pier

2223 Folly Rd., Charleston, SC 29412 (803) 795-4049.

This pier is on Folly Creek. Length: 80 feet. Open year-round. Bait and tackle shop.

# Appendix B
# Licenses and Regulations

## Licenses

### North Carolina

North Carolina currently has no requirement for any form of sport fishing license or stamp for marine waters, although this matter is under consideration and a decision is expected in 1995.

### South Carolina

If you are fishing for marine finfish from a privately owned boat in South Carolina salt waters you need a South Carolina Marine Recreational Fisheries Stamp, unless you meet these exceptions: you are under 16 years of age; are a resident of South Carolina with a valid Gratis Over 65 or Gratis Disability driver's license; a resident on military leave and stationed outside the state; or are a 100 per cent permanently disabled veteran.

You need no stamp or license to fish from a permitted pier, bridge, shore, dock or other land-based structure, or from a permitted charter or head boat.

This stamp costs $5.50 (resident or non-resident), and can be purchased from any of the 170 licensing agents along the coast, such as bait and tackle shops, hardware stores, marinas, sporting good shops, etc. The money goes to the Red Drum Re-stocking Program, Artificial Reef Development, Public Shellfish Ground Enhancement, and other important programs that enhance the fisheries.

These regulations were in effect in the spring of 1994, and, of course, are subject to change. For more information, contact: S.C. Wildlife and Marine Resources Dept., PO Box 12559, Charleston, S.C. 29422-2559 or the same agency at PO Box 11710, Columbia, S.C. 29211. You can reach them by telephone at (803) 795-6350 (Charleston) or (803) 734-3838 (Columbia).

# Bag limits

Many species have minimum (and sometimes maximum) length limits, measured as fork length (FL; usually determined as being from the tip of the nose to the fork in the tail) and total length (TL; from the tip of the nose to the very end of the tail). Additionally, daily catch (bag) limits may be in effect. Both the length limits and daily catch limits can change from year to year, so be sure to check current regulations. These were in effect in spring, 1994.

## North Carolina

**Bluefish**: 12 inches (TL). Twenty fish per person per day.

**Cobia:** 33 inches (FL), 37 inches (TL) in state waters, and two fish per person per day; 33 inches (FL) in federal waters and two fish per person per day.

**Flounder**: 13 inches (TL) in state waters with no daily bag limit, 14 inches (TL) in federal waters with a six fish per person per trip bag limit.

**Gray trout**: 10 inches (TL) and ten fish per person per day in state waters.

**Greater amberjack**: 28 inches (FL) in federal waters. No daily bag limit.

**King mackerel**: 20 inches (FL), five fish per person per day in state and federal waters.

**Red drum**: 18 inches (TL) and five fish per person per day in state waters.

**Spanish mackerel**: 12 inches (FL), ten fish per person per day in state and federal waters.

**Spotted seatrout**: 12 inches (TL) and ten fish per person per day in state waters.

**Striped bass:** 18 inches (TL) in inshore waters, 28 inches (TL) in offshore waters. Special daily bag limits may apply—check with DMF (919)726-7021 or 1-800-682-2632 for information.

**Tarpon:** No minimum size limit, one fish per person per day in state waters.

# South Carolina

**Bluefish**: No size limit currently in effect. Ten fish per person per day in state and federal waters.

**Cobia**: 37 inches (TL), 33 inches (FL) in state and federal waters. Two fish per person per day in state and federal waters.

**Flounder**: 12 inches (TL) in state waters. Twenty fish per person per day in state waters.

**Greater amberjack:** 28 inches (FL) in state and federal waters.

**King mackerel**: 20 inches (FL) in state and federal waters. Five fish per person per day.

**Red drum:** 14 inches (TL). Unlawful to possess more than one fish exceeding 32 inches (TL) in state waters. Five fish per person per day in state waters.

**Spanish mackerel:** 14 inches (TL), 12 inches (FL) state and federal waters. Ten fish per person per day in state and federal waters.

**Spotted seatrout:** 12 inches (TL) in state waters. Fifteen fish per person per day in state waters.

**Striped bass**: No size limits in saltwater. Ten fish per person per day. In Wando & Cooper rivers and Santee River downstream to the Intracoastal Waterway, five fish per person per day in state waters.

**Tarpon**: No size limit currently in effect. One fish per person per day in state waters.

# Appendix C
# Bait and Tackle Shops

## North Carolina

## Inland

### Piedmont Triad Region

**Nelson's Bait and Tackle**
821 South Main St., Kernersville, NC 27284 (910) 993-3035 or
1-800-723-5664.

The Nelson clan—Nelson Cowden, Capt. Lee Nelson, and Judy Nelson—
are the proprietors of this establishment known as the Carolina "western
connection" to the coast. Nelson's not only offers a full line of salt-water
tackle, including fly fishing tackle, but has in-house rod and reel repair. They
produce hand-tied rigs, custom salt-water rods, and even arrange guide
service and charters.

### Research Triangle Region

**Nature's Own Sportsman**
740-A East Chatham St., Cary, NC 27511 (919) 467-8803.

Tom Woodruff, owner of Nature's Own Sportsman, carries "just about
everything for the fisherman," stocking rods, reels, accessories, lures and live
bait for both salt-water and fresh-water fishing. His shop is an authorized
service center for Minn Kota trolling motors. Tom also services in-house four
of the top reels used on the coast: Penn, Shimano, Daiwa, and Garcia.

**Retail Hunting & Fishing**
Rt. 4, Box 477B, Hwy. 70 East, Durham, NC 27703 (919) 596-2455.

Mel Royal and Sidney Lowe have salt-water bait and tackle, including live
bait. They also repair rods and reels.

# Coastal

## Outer Banks

**Hatteras Harbor Marina**, Hatteras Island (919) 986-2166.

**Fishing Unlimited Seafood & Tackle Shop**, Nags Head-Manteo Causeway (919) 441-7040 or (919) 441-5028.

**Pirate's Cove Yacht Club**, Manteo (919) 473-3906.

**Red Drum Tackle Shop**, Hwy 12, Buxton (919) 995-5414.

**Frisco Rod & Gun**, Hwy 12, Frisco (919) 995-5366.

## Morehead City Region

**Aaron's Discount Bait & Tackle**, Atlantic Beach Causeway, Atlantic Beach (919) 240-3474.

Aaron's has a huge selection of live and frozen bait—probably the largest in the state—including fiddler crabs, ballyhoo, squid, minnows, mullet, and worms. Charters also can be arranged here.

**Capt. Joe Shute's Bait & Tackle**, Atlantic Beach Causeway, Atlantic Beach (919) 240-2744 or 1-800-868-0941.

Joe has fresh, frozen and live bait as well as a good selection of rods, reels, and tackle. Joe, who conducts seminars on salt-water fishing, is also available as a guide for inshore light tackle fishing.

**Sea Side Stop-N-Shop & Galley**, Harker's Island (919) 728-5533.

**Dudley's Marina**, Hwy 24 East, Swansboro (919) 393-2204.

**Anchorage Marina**, Atlantic Beach (919) 726-4423.

# Jacksonville Region

**Hunters Corner Sporting Goods**
3059 Gum Branch Rd., Jacksonville, NC  28540 (910) 455-5366.

Nick Fioriti offers tackle for all sorts of salt-water fishing, including fly fishing, but his great selection of seatrout tackle is far wider than that offered by most shops. Nick is also willing to give expert advice and insider tips on what is hitting where, and on what.

# New Bern Region

**New Bern Net Co.**
2703 Hwy. 70 East, New Bern, NC  28562 (919) 633-2226.

Johnie Thompson offers a huge variety of salt-water tackle for inshore and offshore fishing, including fly fishing gear. He also services rods and reels and is happy to offer advice and answer questions.

# Wilmington Region

**Tex's Tackle and Bait**
323 Eastwood Rd., Wilmington, NC  28403 (910) 791-1763.

Tex Grissom has inshore and offshore salt-water tackle, trolling baits, shrimp, mullet, and squid. Tex also carries salt-water fly fishing tackle, including tying materials, and offers professional line winding (for all sizes of reels), custom rigging, special orders, Loran numbers, and tips on hot fishing spots.

**Motts Channel Seafood**, Wrightsville Beach, NC (919) 256-3474.

# South Carolina

## Myrtle Beach Region

**Herb's Bait and Tackle**
911 White Point Rd., North Myrtle Beach, SC  29582 (803) 272-6632.

There used to be a pier with this shop, but Hurricane Hugo stole it. Herb

Burns, who now owns it, offers an excellent selection of rods and reels, including a full line of popular Penn reels. Daiwa, Silstar (a rising name, but still behind in drag systems), Master (a no-frills name) and some Eagle Claw gear are also available. Herb also offers all types of frozen and cut bait and live bait including mud minnows, finger mullet, shrimp, and worms.

**Booty's Fishing and Marine Supplies**, Hwy 17 (Business), Murrell's Inlet (803) 651-2593.

**Inlet Bait and Tackle**, Hwy 17 (Business), Murrell's Inlet (803)651-9166.

## Beaufort Region

**Lemon Island Marina**, Hwy 170, Beaufort (803) 521-9222.

**Driftwood Bait Shop**, Hwy 21, Grays Hill (803) 846-6891.

**Mud Bar Seafood**, Hwy 170, Beaufort (803) 521-9292.

**Bob White's**, Hwy 170 at Hwy 128, Hilton Head (803) 726-5352.

## Charleston Region

**Low Country Marina**, Black Oak Rd., Bonneau (803) 825-6205.

**Water Hole Tackle Shop**, Redbank Rd., Goose Creek (803) 572-6542.

**Pappy's Sportsman Center**, Hwy 52, Goose Creek (803) 553-8725.

**Ravenel ACE Hardware**, Hwy 17 at Hwy 165, Ravenel (803) 889-9176.

**Folly Road Tackle Shop**, 805 Folly Rd., Charleston (803) 762-7397.

**Crosby's Fish & Shrimp Co.**, 2223 Folly Rd., Charleston (803)795-4049.

**Haddrell's Point Tackle & Supply**, Coleman Blvd., Mt. Pleasant (803) 881-3644.

**Toler's Cove Marina**, Mt. Pleasant, (803) 881-0325.

**Jabo's Bait & Tackle**, Hwy 17A at Hwy 61, Summerville (803)851-3341.

# Appendix D
# Environmental Organizations

Several groups are fighting to save the precious marine resources we have left. They do battle with companies, governmental bodies, institutions and other groups and individuals who seek to alter the coastal environment.

One battle underway as I write is with Texasgulf, which operates a huge phosphate mine in North Carolina's Beaufort County. The company is trying to secure a permit to expand its operations in that region. Their permit application has five alternatives outlined in the Draft Environmental Impact Statement, and Texasgulf wants Alternative B, which would damage or destroy 3,069 wetlands over hundreds of acres.

This, by the way, is the same outfit with the clever television ad that ends up with a happy little duckling swimming in a pool of clear water with the Texasgulf logo splashed across the bottom.

Unfortunately, the Army Corps of Engineers, which has a despicable record on environmental matters, is the agency that will grant or deny this permit.

The primary organization fighting to keep this permit from being issued is the Pamlico-Tar River Foundation, whose president, Ben Brinson, knows all too well the history of Texasgulf and the Corps of Engineers. This group deserves your support. The address: PO Box 1854, Washington, N.C. 27889. Telephone: 919-946-7211.

## Other Groups Working to Save the Coastal Environment

**League of Conservation Voters**
Executive Director: Jim Maddy
1707 L St NW, Suite 550
Washington, DC 20036
(202)785-8683

This non-partisan organization gathers and disseminates voting records of Washington politicians, among other things. It lists both of North Carolina's senators—Jesse Helms and Lauch Faircloth—and three members of the

House—Cas Ballenger, Alex McMillan, and Howard Coble—as having dismal voting records on pro-environmental issues. South Carolina's Senator Strom Thurmond, whose record is among the worst, and Thomas Spence in the House are also on the list. These seven politicians need to be sent packing.

## Center for Marine Conservation
President: Roger McManus
1725 DeSales St NW, Suite 500
Washington, DC 20036
(202)429-5609

CMC is heavily into coastal resources protection at all levels. The center specializes in the recovery of endangered or threatened species and fish populations, habitat conservation, and pollution abatement.

## Clean Water Action
Executive Director: David Zwick
1320 Eighteenth St NW
Washington, DC 20036
(202)457-1286

Clean Water Action is one of the largest (600,000 members) environmental action groups devoted to protecting our waters, serving as a watchdog on polluters of all sorts. It was a driving force behind the Clean Air and Clean Water Acts.

## Coastal Conservation Association, Inc.
Executive Director: Ray Poage
4801 Woodway, Suite 220 West
Houston, TX 77056
(713)626-4222

This group is smaller but very active in stopping destruction of coastal resources.

**Coastal Society**
Executive Director: Thomas Bigford
PO Box 2081
Gloucester, MA 01930-2081
(508)281-9209

The Coastal Society conducts workshops and conferences promoting the protection and restoration of coastal resources.

**Cousteau Society**
Executive Vice-President: Jean-Michel Cousteau
930 West 21st St
Norfolk, VA 23517
(804)627-1144

The name alone draws many members. Founded by the famous explorer and scientist Jacques-Yves Cousteau and now run by his son Jean-Michel, the Cousteau Society works through many means to save our waters and coasts.

# Other Organizations

These groups are not focused on marine resources but are worthy of your consideration.

**Citizens Clearinghouse for Hazardous Waste**
PO Box 6806, Falls Church, VA 22040, (703)237-2249

**Ducks Unlimited**
One Waterfowl Way, Memphis, TN 38190, (901)775-3825

**Earth Island Institute**
300 Broadway, Suite 28, San Francisco, CA 94133, (415)788-3666

**Environmental Action Inc.**
6930 Carroll Ave, Suite 600, Takoma Park, MD 20912, (301)891-1100

**Environmental Defense Fund**
257 Park Ave South, New York, NY 10010, (212)505-2100

**Izaak Walton League**
1401 Wilson Blvd, Level B, Arlington, VA 22209, (703)528-1818

**National Toxics Campaign**
1168 Commonwealth Ave, Boston, MA 02134, (617)232-0327

**Natural Resources Defense Council**
40 West 20th St, New York, NY 10011, (212)727-2700

**Nature Conservancy**
1815 North Lynn St, Arlington, VA 22209, (703)841-5300

**US Public Interest Research Group**
215 Pennsylvania Ave SE, Washington, DC 20003, (202)546-9707

**Acid Rain Foundation**
1410 Varsity Dr, Raleigh, NC 27606, (919)828-9443

**Cenozoic Society**
68 Riverside Dr, Apt 1, Canton, NY 13617, (315)379-9940

**Center for Environmental Information**
46 Prince St, Rochester, NY 14607, (716)271-3550

**National Wetlands Technical Council**
1616 P St NW, Suite 200, Washington, DC 20036, (202)328-5150

**Water Pollution Control Federation**
601 Whythe St, Alexandria, VA 22314, (703)684-2400

**World Resources Institute**
1709 New York Ave NW, Washington, DC 20006, (202)638-6300

# Federal Agencies Dealing With Coastal Resources

**US Dept of Agriculture**
Fourteenth St and Independence Ave SW, Washington, DC 20250
(202)447-2791

**Army Corps of Engineers**
Pulaski Bldg, 20 Massachusetts Ave NW, Washington, DC 20314
(202)272-0001

**Dept. of Environmental Protection**
401 M St SW, Washington, DC 20460, (202)382-2090

**National Marine Fisheries Service**
Silver Spring Metro Center 1, 1335 East-West Hwy, Silver Spring,
MD 20910, (301)427-2239

# U.S. Congressional Committees

**US Senate**
Committee on Energy and Natural Resources
Room SD-364, Dirksen Bldg, Washington, DC 20510, (202)224-4971

# Appendix E
# Guides, Charter Boats, and Head (Party) Boats

## North Carolina

### Guides and Charters

### Inland

#### Research Triangle Region

Capt. Bill Harris (specializing in saltwater fly fishing for trophy cobia, seatrout, drum, blues, and stripers); (919) 489-8504 or (919) 419-0552.

Bill, one of the most experienced saltwater fly anglers in North Carolina, is based in Durham but fishes the Crystal Coast.

### Coastal

#### Outer Banks

**Brian Horsley** (specializing in saltwater fly fishing); (919) 261-1541.

**Capt. Rick Caton** (specializing in light tackle tarpon); (919) 473-1209.

**Capt. David Swain**; (919) 473-3386.

**Capt. R.T. O'Neal Jr.**; (919) 928-4841.

## Morehead City Region

**Capt. Joe Shute** (specializing in puppy drum, cobia, and seatrout); (919) 240-2744 or 1-800-868-0941.

Joe is renowned for his ability to find big fish inshore.

**Capt. J.A. Dibella**; (919) 240-2128 or (919) 726-8555. Cape Lookout Guide Service (specializing in drum, seatrout, whiting, flounder, spanish mackerel and blues); (910) 599-6682.

**Capt. Sonny Rains**; 1-800-445-2055.

## Wilmington Region

**Capt. Mike King**; (919) 458-3348 or (919) 540-7174.

**Capt. Chuck Harrill**; (910) 458-4362 or 1-800-288-3474.

# Head (Party) Boats

## Outer Banks

**Crystal Dawn**; (919) 473-5577.

## Morehead City Region

**Capt. Stacy IV**; (919) 247-7501 or 1-800-533-9417.

**Continental Shelf**; (919) 726-7454 or 1-800-775-7450.

## Surf City Region

**Blue Heron II**; (910) 327-1081.

# South Carolina

# Guides and Charters

## Charleston Region

**J.J.W. Luden and Company**; Concord and Charlotte Sts., Charleston (803) 723-7829.

Run by Bramblett Bradham and chief guide Capt. Richard Stuhr, this group specializes in year-round fishing for redfish in the Charleston region, the Ace River Basin, and the Cape Romain Wildlife Refuge where drum up to 40 pounds sometimes roam the shallows in schools of 200 or more. Guides are also available for fishing tarpon, spanish mackerel, ladyfish, crevalle jack, trout and flounder.

**Blue Boy Sportfishing Charters**; (803) 571-1830 or (803) 571-2583.

**Sea Fix Charters**; (803) 577-0800 or (803) 881-0180.

**Haddrell's Point Guide Service** (through Haddrell's Point Tackle & Supply); (803) 881-3644.

# Head (Party) Boats

## Charleston Region

**Carolina Clipper**; (803) 884-2992 or (803) 881-0132.

# Appendix F
# Marinas and Boat Dealers

## North Carolina

### Outer Banks

**Manteo Marine**; Manteo (919) 579-2781

### Morehead City Region

**Power Marine Outfitters**; on the Atlantic Intracoastal Waterway, Sneads Ferry (910) 327-3953

**Walsh Marine**; Hwy 70, Havelock (919) 447-2277

**Atlantic Beach Causeway Marina**; Atlantic Beach (919) 726-6977

**70 West Marina**; Morehead City (919) 726-5171

**Jones Brothers Marine**; Hwy 70 West, Morehead City (919) 726-8404

**HMY Marine Sales**; Hwy 70 West, Morehead City (919) 247-6900

**Wheels & Keels**; Hwy 58, Cape Carteret (919) 393-2011 or 393-6655

**Coastal Marine & Sports**; 1307 NC 58, Cape Carteret (919) 393-7044

**Town Creek Yacht Sales**; West Beaufort Rd., Beaufort (919) 728-6111

**Radio Island Marina**; Beaufort (919) 247-3672

**Fort Macon Marina**; Atlantic Beach (919) 726-3097

**Morehead Marine**; Hwy 70 West, Morehead City (919) 247-6667

**Boats, Inc.**; Hwy 70 West, Morehead City (919) 726-2196

**Caspers Drystack & Marine**; Hwy 24, Swansboro (910) 326-4462

**Jim Bailey's Coral Bay Marina**; Morehead City (919) 247-4231

**Jim Bailey's Crow's Nest Marina**; Morehead City (919) 726-4048

**Dudley's Marine, Inc.**; Hwy 24, Swansboro (910) 393-2204

**Morehead Sports Marina**; Morehead City (919) 726-5676

**Tideline Marine**; Kerr St., Jacksonville (910) 455-2979

**Pamlico Marine**; New Bern (919) 637-1717

**Power Craft Marine**; Oriental (919) 249-2660

**Morehead Gulf Docks** (The Dock Shop); Morehead City Waterfront (919) 726-5461

**Beaufort Gulf Docks**; Beaufort Waterfront (919) 728-6000

## Surf City Region

**Power Marine Outfitters**; on the AIW, Sneads Ferry (910) 327-3953

**New River Marina**; on the New River, Sneads Ferry (910) 327-2106

## Wilmington Region

**Crocker's Marine**; Wrightsville Beach (910) 256-3661

**Page's Creek Marine**; Market St., Wilmington (910) 799-7179

**Bradley Creek Marina**; Oleander Dr., Wilmington (910) 350-0660

**Clanton Offshore Yachts**; Sunset Beach (910) 579-2781

# South Carolina

## Myrtle Beach Region

**Hague Marina**; PO Box 835, Myrtle Beach (803) 293-2141

**Coquina Harbor Marina**; PO Box 4068, N. Myrtle Beach (803) 249-5376

**Wacca Wachee Marina**; PO Box 570, Murrell's Inlet
(803) 651-7171/651-2994

**Harbor Gate Marina Village**; PO Box 3197, N. Myrtle Beach (803) 249-8888

**North Myrtle Beach Marina**; Hwy 90, N. Myrtle Beach (803) 249-1222

**Vereen's Marina**; PO Box 70, N. Myrtle Beach (803) 249-4333

**Bucksport Plantation Marina**; Rt. 1, Bucksport (803) 397-5566

**Little River Plantation Marina**; PO Box 365, Little River
(803) 249-5294/249-4735

**Briarcliffe RV Resort and Yacht Club**; 10495 Kings Hwy, Myrtle Beach
(803) 272-4332

## Georgetown Region

**Georgetown Landing Marina**; PO Box 1704, Georgetown (803) 546-1776

**Belle Isle Marina**; PO Box 796, Georgetown (803) 546-8491

**Exxon Marina**; 18 S. James St., Georgetown (803) 546-4370

**Gulf Auto Marina**; 525 Front St., Georgetown (803) 546-4250

**Hazard's Marina**; Georgetown (803) 546-6604

# Charleston Region

**Darby Marine and Supply**; PO Box 188, Mt. Pleasant (803) 884-8541

**Stono Marina**; 2409 Maybank Hwy, Johns Island (803) 559-2307

**Ashley Marina**; 33 Lockwood Blvd., Charleston (803) 772-1996

**George M. Lockwood Municipal Marina**; 17 Lockwood Blvd., Charleston (803) 577-6970

**Wild Dunes Yacht Harbor**; PO Box 527, Isle of Palms (803) 886-5100

**Bohicket Marina**; 1880 Andell Bluff Rd., Johns Island (803) 768-1280

**Buzzard's Roost Marina**; 2408 Maybank Hwy, Johns Island (803) 559-5516

**Toler's Cove Marina**; 1610 Hwy 703, Mt. Pleasant (803) 881-0325

**Shem Creek Marina**; 526 Mill St., Mt. Pleasant (803) 884-3211

**Duncan's Boat Harbor**; 1997 Bridge View Dr., Charleston Heights (803) 744-2628

**Northbridge Marina**; 2079 Austin Ave., Charleston (803) 744-2562

**Cast-A-Way Texaco Marina**; 101 Palm Blvd., Isle of Palms (803) 886-4396

**Leland Marine Services, Inc.**; PO Box 357, McClellanville (803) 887-3641

# Beaufort Region

**Skull Creek Marina**; PO Box 2047, Hilton Head (803) 681-4234

**Shelter Cove Marina**; PO Box 5628, Hilton Head (803) 842-7001

**Harbor Town Yacht Basin**; Lighthouse Rd., Hilton Head Island (803)671-2704

**Windmill Harbor Marina**; 161 Harbor Passage, Hilton Head (803) 681-9235

**Palmetto Bay Marine Center;** 164 Palmetto Bay, Hilton Head (803) 785-3910

**Port Royal Landing Marina**; PO Drawer 1257, Beaufort (803) 525-6664

**Downtown Marina of Beaufort**; 1010 Bay St., Beaufort (803) 524-4422

**Marsh Harbor Marina**; Beaufort (803) 524-4797

**Outdoor Resorts Marina**; Hilton Head Island (803) 681-3241